Soul Deep
Exploring Spirituality Together

An Eight-week Course for Small Groups

Michael Allured and Kate Dean

The Lindsey Press
London

the unitarians

Published by the Lindsey Press
on behalf of the General Assembly of
Unitarian and Free Christian Churches
Essex Hall, 1–6 Essex Street, London WC2R 3HY, UK

www.unitarian.org.uk

© General Assembly of Unitarian and Free Christian Churches 2024

ISBN 978-0-85319-100-1

Designed and typeset by Garth Stewart
Front-cover image created by Stewart Dean

Michael Allured is the minister serving Golders Green Unitarians, in north-west London. Before training for ministry he had a full-time career in the Civil Service, which he now combines for part of the week with Unitarian ministry. Michael is a keen meditator and during the Covid pandemic he began offering daily online meditation sessions to his Civil Service colleagues. He is currently (2024) the Chair of the governing council of Unitarians in London and the South East and serves on the committee of the Unitarian Peace Fellowship and on the Hucklow Summer School panel. He is married to Revd Feargus O'Connor, a fellow Unitarian minister, who is equally crazy about cats.

Kate Dean is the minister at Rosslyn Hill Unitarian Chapel, an open-minded spiritual community in Hampstead, north-west London. She holds an MA in Abrahamic Religions. She has a creative background, having studied product design at University, and has organised several creativity and spirituality groups. Before training to be a minister, she worked in toy and games design, project management, and youth work. She has co-led many engagement groups with her congregation, and at the annual Hucklow Summer School, an all-ages Religious Education programme for the Unitarians. She lives in Hampstead with her husband and young son.

We are physical entities. But we are also people with emotions, talents, passions: people of spirit on a journey of discovery. What is it that we seek? And how, if we are free spirits unbound by the creeds and dogmas of organised and codified world religions, do we find the essence of truth, peace, and wholeness that we desire?

Our individual study and the development of a regular spiritual practice take us only so far. We are not made to live and learn, grow and develop, in isolation. We need the support and discipline of exploring our own spiritual journey and our search for meaning in community. It is the work of the soul that we do with others that provides a backdrop to the canvas on which our spiritual journey is created.

Contents

Acknowledgements   ix

Introduction   1

Part 1: Why are small groups important?   5

Part 2: Weekly Sessions   13

    Week 1: Finding purpose, meaning, and identity   14

    Week 2: Our need for connection   24

    Week 3: The big questions, Part 1   31

    Week 4: The big questions, Part 2   37

    Week 5: What gets in the way?, Part 1   45

    Week 6: What gets in the way?, Part 2   53

    Week 7: Finding ways to deepen our soul connections   61

    Week 8: Wrap-up. Gathering and bringing in the harvest   69

Part 3: Facilitator's Guidelines   85

Appendix (i): Group covenant   110

Appendix (ii): Extra readings   116

Appendix (iii): Extra activities   131

Appendix (iv): Sample promotion text   145

Appendix (v): Sample follow-up invitation   146

Appendix (vi): Contributors   148

Acknowledgements

First, we would like to thank The Lindsey Press for commissioning us to produce this engagement-group course, which was inspired by the online series of Soul Deep engagement-group gatherings that we co-facilitated during 2020 and 2021. We are indebted to all those who offered their own poetry and prose contributions: Yvonne Aburrow, Jane Blackall, Jeffrey Bowes, Celia Cartwright, Rory Castle Jones, Bert Clough, Aria Datta, Judith Fantozzi, Winnie Gordon, Linda Hart, Jo James, Roger Mason, Ayndrilla Singharay, Adam Slate, and Sally Somerville. Our warmest thanks to everyone who offered contributions. Without your help this engagement-group resource would not be what it has become. We are especially grateful to Revd Dr Jane Blackall and Adam Slate for reviewing the guidelines for facilitators and providing valuable and thoughtful perspectives. We also give our thanks to Feargus O'Connor and Charles Groome for reviewing and proofreading the manuscript.

Introduction

This course is intended for anyone who is committed to a path of developing spiritual practices, as an individual and with others in community, to arrive at a deeper understanding of themselves and each other. It is soul work. We cannot promise that embarking on spiritual journeys will be easy, but we aspire to make it an experience that enriches self-knowledge and shows us, through our shared stories and deep listening, that there are experiences and feelings that we have in common, in spite of our diversity.

While it is possible to use this book's resources for personal study and reflection, the course is primarily intended for use in small groups. The ideal size of group would be from six to eight people, with a maximum of twelve. This is in order to get the most from the course by giving sufficient time for participants to connect and share personal stories and experiences in a safe and non-judgemental space.

The process of creating this course has been a delight. At the heart of our intention was the desire to provide an accessible resource that gives seekers (whether or not committed to a particular faith tradition) a space in which to grapple with the deeper questions, philosophical and practical, that we need to talk about in much greater depth. What is my place in the Universe, and how do I begin to discover it? What are my 'soul anchors', and how can I find them and put them to good use? We wanted to respond to a strongly perceived need for people to feel connected to others and nurtured by a sense of belonging with a group of like-minded free spirits.

Andrei Sakharov, the Soviet human-rights campaigner, expressed it well when he observed: 'I am unable to imagine the Universe and human life without some guiding principle, without a source of spiritual "warmth" which is non-material and not bound by physical laws.' Many who identify as 'spiritual but not religious' are likely to have similar feelings. This course is one response to that need. It is offered as a way in to starting those deeper conversations.

According to Julianne Holt-Lunstad, a professor of psychology and neuroscience who studies aspects of loneliness, 'our social relationships are widely considered crucial to emotional well-being; however, the possibility that social connection may be a biological need, vital to physical well-being and even survival, is commonly unrecognised'. And although Western society is becoming increasingly secular, research suggests that many individuals would nevertheless describe themselves as 'spiritual' but not 'religious'.

Professor Michael King from King's College London suggests that approximately one fifth of people in the UK identify in this way. But what does it mean? Some would describe it as a 'feeling' that there is 'something else'. Science may take us a long way in explaining the world – to the extent that there is even current speculation about whether a robot programmed by artificial intelligence (AI) can actually be sentient. But science does not explain how so many people feel about their place in the Universe, their feelings of awe and wonder at the sight of a sunset, or the 'tingle factor' that might be activated when listening to a particular piece of music.

Some believe that codified religion is a human construct that can divide us, and a product of culture related to time and place. Spirituality, on the other hand, speaks to 21st-century Western minds in a language that is more accessible because it helps to make sense of basic feelings that are universal to humanity. It gives our lives a deeper meaning. Notwithstanding cultural differences, the instincts of love, fear, grief, joy, and sadness evoke the same recognisable feelings in humans everywhere.

This course of spiritual exploration consists of eight sessions, each lasting two hours. The structure of each session is designed to encourage opportunities for personal reflection and small-group work in response to short texts on the theme of the session. The intention is to offer a 'holding space' for participants to do 'soul work' within a structure that gives them time to reflect on how they find meaning and fulfilment of the spirit, and to be nourished by listening to the shared experiences of others. Each of the sessions invites participants to engage with a theme that deals with a particular aspect of the spiritual journey. We begin by exploring identity and acknowledging our need to feel connected to the world around us. We then move on to consider our responses to some of life's 'big questions' about living and dying. We conclude with exploring the aspects of life which might get in the way of our tending to our spiritual journey.

Each session plan provides a structure to guide participants as they engage with the theme through personal and shared reflection. Each session includes suggested readings to help that process. There are additional readings and activities organised by session theme in Appendix (ii) and Appendix (iii). We have also written a special section for facilitators of the course, with the intention of enabling both facilitators and participants to have a richly rewarding experience. Based on our own experiences of facilitating small groups, and on the experiences of our colleagues, we have included information about the facilitator's role, advice about planning for each session, and tips and guidance on a variety of general aspects of leading small groups.

As we acknowledge the busyness of our lives in the modern world, we intend the course to help participants to explore what gets in the way of 'soul work', so that they can find ways of deepening their spiritual practice as individuals and in communities as they journey towards finding connection with other people on a similar quest for wholeness. Whether participants are already members of a Unitarian community or are still searching for opportunities to explore spirituality more deeply, we aspire to give people a practical structure through which to develop their spiritual lives.

Thank you for choosing to engage with *Soul Deep*. May it be a journey of discovery, affirmation, and healing.

Part 1: Why are small groups important?

Digging more deeply to explore eternal questions

The traditional Sunday service that remains the main feature of many, if not all, religious communities in the Christian tradition and associated free-thinking communities will not, for a range of different reasons, have universal appeal. Some congregations have added extra activities to their programmes, designed to stimulate explorations of aspects of spirituality and religion in small groups. Within Unitarian communities these groups are sometimes called 'Engagement Groups',[1] 'Small Group Ministry', or 'Chalice Circles'. Small-group work of this nature is held within a structure that has an opening and closing, and a series of prepared activities that are the main content.

Small-group work, well facilitated, can create a different energy from that of a traditional Sunday service. It can be an exciting form of outreach to spiritual seekers. This format can help to create the conditions for deeper connection among people who meet regularly at church but have never had an opportunity to share their spiritual journey in a deeper way. This model for exploring life's deeper questions may be particularly enriching for small congregations if they decide to experiment with a group-like format instead of a formal service. This format can not only open up new perspectives for established members of religious communities but can also be used to revitalise a small congregation.

1   This model for exploring spirituality was introduced to Unitarian communities in the UK when a Unitarian Universalist theologian, Thandeka, gave a keynote lecture at the Unitarian Annual Meetings in 2002.

Creating safe space for spiritual exploration and growth

It has been said that small groups like these are meant to bring us into 'right relationship' with ourselves, each other, and the Universal Spirit of Life whom some of us know as God. They are a way of nurturing our own spiritual development through the deepening of connections within a community where we grow a sense of belonging. We receive some information passively through talks, worship services, and lectures. In contrast, engagement groups prompt us to interact with the topic material at a deeper level: we have space for quiet reflection and are able to gain wider perspectives and insights through our own deep listening to what other members of the group choose to share. We pay close attention to the ways in which we interact with each other as we model the spiritual practice of speaking and listening with care.

Over the years we have led many groups using the 'engagement group' approach that will be described here. Participants have told us about their experience of the process. They spoke about feeling nourished and connected, finding common ground, and leaving feeling lighter.

This process of engagement may be new to people who have not experienced working in a small group as a way of exploring spirituality and religion. The format for each two-hour session in this course offers a structured framework that helps the facilitator to guide participants through each of the activities. The intention of this course is to enable participants (who may or may not know each other) to make much deeper connections than are possible at coffee time after a Sunday service. In this way people are able to build relationships with other members of the group and therefore create bonds of friendship, with a sense of belonging to a community that inspires them to keep returning because of the energy and connection generated by the 'soul work' that they do alone and together.

Offering an alternative way to engage with life's big questions

We often hear people say that they had never heard of Unitarians until, from necessity, they were looking for an inclusive church to celebrate a birth or a marriage, or to mark the death of a loved one. Others, on discovering a Unitarian community, have commented that it offers a way of feeding the soul for which they had been searching over many years.

Anita, a woman in late middle age, appeared in the entrance of a Unitarian chapel one Sunday and was unsure, when the minister greeted her, whether or not to go in. She had 'gone off' religion because, she said, 'No one was prepared to answer any questions; no one was prepared to discuss them.' She recalls fondly that when she confessed to the minister that she didn't believe in the divinity of Christ and he replied that nor did he, and invited her in, she was 'hooked'. Although she admitted to not being a 'joiner', she soon applied for membership.

What brought her to the doors of a Unitarian chapel on that spring Sunday? Clearly she was searching for meaning. One could have seen her as 'a lost soul' seeking more satisfying (if incomplete) answers to questions about universal issues, the span of life, the joys and sorrows of humanity, and perhaps especially the meaning of her own life. Deep down, Anita was lonely. Something was missing. She sought understanding, empathy, a sense of belonging among people where she felt she was understood and accepted. She found it in a Unitarian community.

How many more Anitas are there? Figures from the British Red Cross suggest that more than 9 million adults in the UK are often or always lonely. Loneliness affects people of all ages, but, according to Age UK, 3.6 million people aged 65 and over regard the television as their main form of company. According to Carers UK, '8 out of 10 carers have felt lonely or isolated as a result of looking after a loved one'. The

Campaign to End Loneliness found that many family doctors estimate that a fifth of the people they see have come because they are lonely. It's sad to think that consulting their GP is a social interaction which some patients don't feel they can get elsewhere.

Engagement-group courses such as this are opportunities to offer something precious to the world by welcoming those who are lost and lonely and in search of meaning. Unitarian communities across the UK have the potential to help create and strengthen these bonds of connection between seekers in their joy and pain. A hymn by the Quaker poet John Greenleaf Whittier speaks of worship that 'restores the lost, binds up the spirit broken'. Within the framework of small-group engagement may we aspire to do that for ourselves and each other.

Using the 'engagement group' approach

Engagement groups help participants to deepen their spiritual life and their connections with each other. Their purpose is to cultivate 'right relationship' with self, with each other, and with whatever conception they have of the Divine, which some may name God. They are a chance to create a greater sense of community through individual and shared reflection, and to practise essential deep listening skills which are often missing in our usual daily experiences.

The structure of the sessions presented in the book is based on the 'engagement group' model which has been used at the British Unitarian Religious Education residential Summer School in Great Hucklow, and at many other Unitarian events for decades. In the words of Revd Dr Jane Blackall:

> There are principles which make small groups healthy. These principles are the values we cherish as Unitarians: human dignity, reverence for life, the democratic process, compassion, the free search for truth, loving kindness, justice, and equality.

9

We live these values in our small groups as a spiritual experience. The 'Light' or 'God' or 'highest goodness' within each person is encouraged to come out and be shared with the group.[2]

She has outlined practical skills and qualities which help small groups to be successful. These include:

- Non-judgemental sharing

- The 'pass' option: active participation by free choice in response to an invitation

- Clear leadership

- A chance for everyone to participate

- An openness to diversity

- A minimum of cross-talking and an absence of arguing

- Speaking one's truth with respect, and listening to another with respect

- Acceptance of the value of silence

- Clarity about the Unitarian values that we cherish and agree to abide by

- A safe meeting space

- Clear time guidelines

2   Quoted from a document entitled 'Engagement Groups in a Nutshell' by Jane Blackall.

Soul Deep session structure

Each session of this course includes the following elements:

- Opening rituals: chalice-candle lighting, opening words of welcome
- Brief check-in by each participant (prompted, for example, by 'How is your heart this evening?')
- Activities: contemplative shared reading and response with the whole group
- Individual writing, meditation, or other activity
- Deeper sharing in small groups
- Check-out by each person (prompted, for example, by 'What will you take home from this evening?')
- Closing rituals: words and/or music.

The importance of a group agreement or covenant

To ensure that all participants get what they need from an engagement group, and to help everyone feel safe and heard as we do soul work, it is important for everyone in the group to agree on the ways in which they want to be together and engage with each other.

The usual practice for facilitating these guidelines is for the group to agree to a set of statements. The most familiar term to describe these 'promises' to each other is 'group covenant'. These statements are ones that the group agrees to uphold in order to create a safe, fertile, and inclusive space for spiritual exploration. Every group is encouraged to agree on a covenant that defines how participants will engage with and relate to each other. It includes approaches to speaking, listening, respecting confidentiality, and other group behaviours. A list of covenants has been used by other Unitarian engagement groups, and a full explanation of the reason behind each is available in Appendix (i). Group covenants are considered in more detail in the first session.

The facilitator's role

To get the most out of *Soul Deep*, we recommend that the group's progress is facilitated. A facilitator serves as a guide and host for the group, to help participants embark on a journey of self-awareness and spiritual growth. The facilitator plays a valuable leadership role in 'holding' the group and helping it to uphold the engagement-group principles and covenant. A facilitator ensures that the session is clearly structured and flows smoothly, while keeping track of time and ensuring that everyone's voice is heard. In Part 3 facilitators will find comprehensive guidance for reference and support as they plan for the next eight weeks.

In the outlines of the weekly sessions, instructions for facilitators are flagged by tick-boxes and bullet points. Participants can skip these bits and focus on the readings, while the facilitator guides them through the activities. Participants, trust yourselves and the group to be held by your facilitator, so they can help you get what you need from *Soul Deep* by creating a safe and inspiring space for you all to learn from each other.

Engaging with other people through small-group work is a journey that can become an exciting adventure. May the spiritual journey that you choose to embark upon through this course be an adventure that is an enriching experience, rewarding your trust and faith in the process of discovery.

Part 2:
Weekly Sessions

 # Week 1: Finding purpose, meaning, and identity

Preparation for facilitators

You will need:

- Any music that you intend to play, and the means with which to play it

- A box of tissues

- A large copy of the Group Covenant Summary from Appendix (i) on display (optional)

- Spare paper and pens for any participants who don't have a notebook

Chalice-candle lighting and silence (3 minutes)

☐ If the group is meeting in person, arrange chairs in a circle. If it's an online meeting, choose the 'gallery view' option so that all the participants fit on one screen. You might wish to play some meditative music in the background.

☐ When all are gathered, light the chalice candle, or invite a member of the group to do so.

☐ Then fade the music and invite them all into a time of stillness.

> **Opening words:** *We Gather As Pilgrims* by Michael Allured
>
> We gather as pilgrims, each on our own journey and together on a shared adventure. We cannot know what is in the heart of another: the pain, the fear, the sorrow, the elation, the joy, the meaning, the peace.
>
> And so we gather together to make heart connections through our shared exploration, in stories, in stillness, and quietly receiving what is offered by each one of us gathered here.
>
> May we hold a shared and safe space for each other: a space for listening with open hearts, a space for finding meaning in our sharing, a space for feeling gratitude.

Check-in (15 minutes)

☐ Invite participants to say their names (and their location if meeting online), and to name a colour that represents how they are feeling right now.

☐ Remind participants that there is a 'pass' option.

☐ If participants are checking in by moving around the circle, you may wish to use a 'talking stick' (an object of your choice) to hold when you are speaking and then pass to the next speaker. Facilitators should be aware of who has spoken and prompt speakers if they don't know whom to nominate next.

☐ Alternatively, participants may prefer to speak as they feel moved to do so by picking up the 'talking stick' when ready to speak, and placing it back in its resting place for the next person when they have finished speaking.

☐ You will want to allow longer for the check-in for Week 1 than in subsequent weeks. To enter straight into a deeper sharing that goes beyond 'How are you?' and to create the tone for the session, participants could be invited to respond to the question 'How is your heart today?'

Overview of the course (10 minutes)

Introduce the course and remind participants what they should expect during the eight-week course. Set the scene by including the following:

☐ Welcome to *Soul Deep*, a Unitarian course to help us in our spiritual quest.

☐ Set out the course intention: over eight weeks the intention is to go on a shared journey to deepen our spiritual practice and reflection. We are creating time for ourselves and each other, in a safe, non-judgemental space, to explore the questions that matter to us in life and which give our lives meaning.

☐ Explain the format/components for each session (see pages 9–10, 'Engagement-group Approach'). Explain that there will be opportunities for personal reflection and sharing/listening, some of it in smaller break-out groups.

☐ For break-out sessions: people will be in the same group in a single session, e.g. in Week 2 they could be in a different group than in Week 1.

☐ Use a 3-minute or 5-minute timer for people who are sharing personal thoughts.

☐ Mention that each session ends with a check-out sequence, where participants reflect on what they have gained from the experience.

☐ At the first session ask participants if they would like to be part of a WhatsApp group for sharing reflections (but not a debate/discussion) on their responses to particular activities and readings, etc.

☐ Explain the intention to follow 'engagement group' principles. Mention that at the formation of any new engagement group the members agree on guidelines on how to engage with each other. Explain that this is to ensure that everyone feels safe and valued, and that they can contribute as they wish.

☐ Explain that this set of statements is called a 'covenant' – but we don't need to call it that if the group would prefer an alternative, such as 'ways of being together'.

Discussion of group agreement/covenant – or 'ways of being together' (10 minutes)

☐ Take the group through a copy of the long version of the covenant statements (see pages 111–113), with descriptors explaining the rationale behind each principle.

☐ Seek endorsement from the group to adopt the covenant statements. Offer an opportunity for any suggested additions in case there is a principle that is specific to this particular group.

☐ Explain that these are a useful point of reference for how we interact with each other.

☐ Keep a copy of the covenant on display.

Overview of the session (2 minutes)

☐ Remind participants that Week 1 is devoted to exploring how we find meaning and purpose, and the importance of identity. We all do that in diverse ways. In future weeks we will have more time for doing activities and having a discussion.

☐ Explain the overall structure of the session:

- a reading

- a group discussion

- a second reading, followed by an activity that will involve sharing and deep listening in small groups

- a time in the larger group to share insights gained from the deep listening in the small groups

- announcements

- check-out

- closing words

Reading 1: Unlocking A Soul's Potential by Michael Allured

The novelist E. M. Forster famously wrote: 'Only connect'. The capacity to reach out and forge relationships with other people, animals, music, art, and the natural world of which we are all part is an essential human need. We yearn to belong, to fit in, to be of use. That overwhelming desire takes us along all manner of paths: some life-enhancing and others less so. Some of us spend our whole lives struggling to make those longed-for connections. We search for them as we endeavour to shape our lives by trying to find out who we are, what we are meant to do with our lives, and why we are here on this breathtakingly beautiful, awe-inspiring, and yet bloodied, bruised, and aching Planet Earth.

As we make those connections through life, we discover that some are nourishing and help us to blossom, while others drain our spirit and lead us down less healthy paths. Yet, whether the connections that human beings make are life-enhancing or not, the overwhelming need to be wanted is the feeling that most of us live for.

So many of the connections that I myself have made have been life-enhancing. I wonder how many of those connections can be explained by luck – being in the right place at the right time – or by the extent to which, if we believe in such a thing, destiny played a part in them?

As a child I never really fitted in, and that made me wary and fearful of rejection by the fellow human beings in my immediate world and the world at large. I was resigned to leading a solitary and lonely life, and I rarely thought about the future. My main mode of survival was to face the next hurdle as best I could. One Monday in March 1984, the cancellation of my university lecture led me to the canteen, and a four-hour conversation over coffee with my now husband. I didn't know it then, but as I look back I see that this chance meeting was the key to my life path. It was the life event that made possible many other subsequent experiences, including discovering Unitarianism at first hand, and achievements that have been full of meaning and purpose. Some days I still find myself searching for identity and life's meaning and purpose. But I have an anchor. And that makes all the difference.

Group discussion (10 minutes)

☐ Having listened to *Unlocking a Soul's Potential,* you are invited to share your initial thoughts. You might consider the following question:

- What thoughts and feelings does this reading evoke for you about our connections to one another?

Break/music (10 minutes)

Time for a pause from the words, and an opportunity for a comfort break.

Reading 2: *Balance and Flow* by Kate Dean

Since we can't know what lies beyond, we need to make *now* count, through getting the balance right in order to find meaning and purpose in our lives.

Imagine you had to design creatures who can survive on a planet very much like Earth. You would probably want to make the creatures fairly cautious, so they are able to learn from their mistakes, but you would probably also want to give them the curiosity to take a few risks and to be given encouragement if they came up with something new, even if it wasn't immediately useful. This thought experiment was suggested by psychologist Mihaly Csikszentmihalyi [chik-zen-mi-hal-ee] in his book *The Flow of Creativity.*

He suggests that this is exactly what happened in our own evolutionary history. He goes on to write:

It is possible that children who were more curious ran more risks and so were more likely to die earlier than their more stolid companions. But it is also probable that those human groups that learned to appreciate the curious children among them, and helped to protect and reward them so that they could grow to maturity and have children of their own, were more successful than groups that ignored the potentially creative [offspring] in their midst ... We are the descendants of ancestors who recognised the importance of novelty, protected those individuals who enjoyed being creative and learned from them. It made this group better prepared to face unpredictable conditions that threatened their survival.

It is our evolutionary inheritance, then, to use our talents, our curiosity, and creativity in order to bring meaning and purpose in our lives. When I was in my twenties and in search of meaning, an older friend suggested that I use my creativity to write a 'spiritual mission statement'. With the arrogance of youth, it flowed straight out of me! Even decades later, though, I think it is still a good practice to return to, allowing me to reflect on whether I am still on the right path.

Activity (10 minutes) and small-group sharing (20 minutes)

☐ Write a 'spiritual mission statement': one sentence beginning 'I am ...'. (See page 131 for examples.)

☐ Looking back at your younger self, what are the differences between your beliefs then and now?

☐ In small groups of three or four, share your mission statement and your reflections on your younger self; or just say something about your experience of the activity.

☐ In future weeks, we will have time for the small-group responses to be shared with the larger group.

Announcements (2 minutes)

☐ Confirm the date and time of the next meeting.

☐ Explore whether the group would like to do an activity at home. See Appendix (iii) (pages 131–132).

☐ For Week 2, ask participants to bring an object and picture with which they have a special connection.

☐ Remind participants to bring a notebook and their copy of this book next week.

☐ Other housekeeping information.

☐ Invite any questions for clarification.

Check-out (10 minutes)

☐ Invite participants to share a word or phrase about how they are feeling, or what they are taking away from the session.

Closing words: *Clarity Prayer* by Linda Hart

Spirit of love and life,
  within us and around us always,
    in these few moments of quiet and reflection
      we ask for clarity:

  In the comings and goings of our days, may we have the eyes
    to see the manifold blessings that surround us.
      Even in the midst of trouble and worry, may we have the
        ears to hear a sweet song of joy.

Our lives are often a jumble of worry and treasures,
  grant us the clarity
    to know what is worthy and what is not,
      what is noble and what is not,
        what requires our love

And grant us the presence of mind and heart
  to give ourselves to what is worthy and true,
    to give of ourselves to what is noble and blessed,
      to open our hearts to all that is in need of love.

In these few moments at least,
  may we hold what clarity we have,
    and keep it close as we go forward into our days.

So may it be with us all.

Amen

 # Week 2: Our need for connection

Preparation for facilitators

You will need:

- Any music that you intend to play, and the means with which to play it

- A box of tissues

- A large copy of the Group Covenant Summary from Appendix (i) on display (optional)

- Spare paper and pens for any participants who don't have a notebook.

Chalice-candle lighting and silence (3 minutes)

☐ If the group is meeting in person, arrange chairs in a circle. If it's an online meeting, choose the gallery-view option so that all the participants fit on one screen. You might wish to play some meditative music in the background.

☐ Light the chalice candle, or invite a member of the group to do so, when all are gathered.

☐ Then fade the music and invite everyone into a time of stillness.

> **Opening words** by Adam Slate
>
> As we travel the paths that our lives reveal to us,
>
> We often are not sure of the way, the distance, or the destination.
>
> Nevertheless, we have each other.
>
> We can look to one another for wisdom,
>
> We can be grateful for each other's companionship,
>
> And we can seek support when we have lost hope.
>
> May our gathering show our willingness to take the journey together.

Check-in (15 minutes)

☐ Welcome everyone to Week 2 of *Soul Deep* gatherings.

☐ Invite participants to hold up their chosen object and explain briefly why they have brought it. If they have not brought something, they can respond to the question 'How is your heart?'

☐ Remind participants about the pass option.

Overview of session (2 minutes)

☐ Remind everyone about the group agreement and ways of working together that they agreed at the previous session, especially *personal (not general) sharing ... confidentiality ... and deep listening.*

☐ Remind everyone that in Week 2 we will explore our need for connection.

☐ Explain that we make connections in all sorts of ways in relationship to others. And that it is through our connections that we are able to discover life's purpose and meaning through events, objects, and experiences of sadness and joy that create the stories that are the tapestry of our lives.

☐ Suggest that our connections are the threads and branches and roots that are part of our growth, our on-going becoming.

☐ Remind the group of the structure of the session.

Reading 1: *Heart Connection: Sharing is an Answer* by Michael Allured

Whether or not you believe you can sing, singing together can be a truly great therapy. It gets those endorphins surging, to give you a feeling of well-being and a sense that all will be well. When we sing – even if it's only to ourselves – we are reaching out and connecting with another soul, and with the world outside. Through music and song we are telling the world that we are here, and we say to the world: 'I want you to understand my life and the life of my community, and I know that you are here too, and we stand together in empathy and solidarity.' That's true heart connection.

Every musical note that's written and played, every secular and religious song that's sung, is a heart and soul crying out loud to another person in joy and despair, longing and hope. If you listen to Pete Seeger's anthem *We Shall Overcome* or, even better, sing it yourself, either alone or with others, you can feel physical and emotional connection as we sing the lines 'O, deep in my heart, I do believe, We'll walk hand in hand some day'. Here we experience the power to open hearts and build resilience and hope in the face of despair. These words carry a universal message about the need to be together. They've been sung in secular and sacred settings by many people, and we shall keep singing them as we cling to hope.

Another song about connection in the Unitarian hymn book *Sing Your Faith* is number 193, which begins 'We laugh, we cry, we live, we die, we dance, we sing our song'. Its power lies in telling the story of our universal need for connection, and the feeling evoked when we find it. We sing about living together, dancing together, needing to feel there's something to which we can belong. We sing of the need for friends, of dedicating our hearts and minds, the pain of parting from loved ones who die, and the joy of new life. We search with our hearts and finally discover that sharing is an answer.

Singing is good for the soul because it has the power, through rhythm, harmony, and words, to unlock imagination and let in empathy. Without empathy there can be no connection with our fellow human beings or other sentient creatures.

Group discussion (10 minutes)

☐ Invite brief responses to the reading before inviting responses to these questions:

- Can you recall a time when you have experienced a deep feeling of being connected to all life – or a simple feeling of connection?

- Do you find meaning in belonging?

Break/music (15 minutes)

Time for a pause from the words and an opportunity for a comfort break.

Reading 2: *Pain* by Yvonne Aburrow

When pain comes to live in the body
it has a way of taking over my whole awareness,
making me feel trapped in my body with the pain.

But then there's the gratitude
for the love and concern of friends
who wish me well, ask how I am,
some of them reaching out of their own pain
to touch me in healing.

And so my awareness moves
from the pain to my heart
opening in gratitude
for the gift of friends,
sending messages of concern.

A true friend is one who shares
pain and laughter
love and companionship
sorrow and joy.
I give thanks for friends.
I give thanks to friends:
manifestations of divine love.

Activity (10 minutes) and small-group sharing (25 minutes)

☐ Activity: The social critic and feminist, Bell Hooks, wrote: *'Rarely if ever are any of us healed in isolation. Healing is an act of communion.'* Invite participants to re-write this quotation in their notebooks, then make notes on any thoughts or memories that have been prompted by it.

☐ Optional question: When you consider times when you have been in pain, emotionally or physically, how has a sense of isolation or connection affected your progress?

☐ Invite participants, in small groups of three or four, to share their responses to the activity or just say something about their experience of it.

Small-group responses shared with the larger group (5 minutes)

☐ Gather as the full group. Invite people to share with each other a few of the common points or differences that they found in their small groups.

Announcements

☐ Confirm the date and time of the next meeting.

☐ Explain any activity for participants to engage with at home before Week 3.

☐ Remind participants to bring a notebook and their copy of this book next week.

☐ Other housekeeping information.

☐ Invite any questions for clarification.

Check-out (10 minutes)

☐ Invite participants to share a word or phrase about how they are feeling, or what they are taking away from the session.

Closing words by Winnie Gordon

With open hearts and minds we leave,
Remembering we are not alone.
Empowered to be transformed and to transform others.
May the God of your heart guide and protect you as you go on
    your way.
Go in peace and love.
Blessed be and Amen.

Week 3: The big questions

Part 1: Good, evil, suffering, and the nature of God

Preparation for facilitators

You will need:

- Any music that you intend to play, and the means with which to play it.

- A box of tissues.

- A large copy of the Group Covenant Summary from Appendix (i) on display (optional)

- Spare paper and pens for any participants who haven't brought a notebook.

Chalice-candle lighting and silence (3 minutes)

☐ If the group is meeting in person, arrange chairs in a circle. If it's an online meeting, choose the 'gallery view' option so that all the participants fit on one screen. You might wish to play some meditative music in the background.

☐ When all are gathered, light the chalice candle, or invite a member of the group to do so.

☐ Then fade the music and invite them to share a time of stillness.

Opening words by Kate Dean

When we feel weighed down by the world's pain,
it is because we feel it as our own pain, and it can feel overwhelming.
Our hearts can be broken open by the story of a friend,
an article we read about a stranger, or something happening in our
own lives.
It's all we can do not to run away and hide in the face of such suffering.
But we can choose to be present in those moments,
not allowing ourselves to be swallowed up by the horrors.
When we place our faith in something, someone, beyond ourselves,
a path seems to appear in front of us,
and we realise that we are part of something greater,
which holds us and all those around us
in a loving, cosmic embrace.

Check-in (15 minutes)

☐ Welcome everyone to Week 3 of the *Soul Deep* gatherings.

☐ Invite participants to respond to the question *'How is your heart?'*

Overview of session (2 minutes)

☐ Remind everyone about the group agreement and ways of working
together, especially *personal, not general, sharing … confidentiality…
and deep listening.*

☐ Introduce Week 3 as an invitation to explore the nature of God and
begin thinking about the 'big questions': good, evil, notions of an
all-powerful, perfect God or a God still evolving.

☐ Remind the group of the format for the session.

Reading 1: *'Is there an answer to why bad things happen to good people?'* by Michael Allured

In his book *When Bad Things Happen to Good People,* Rabbi Harold S. Kushner wrote: *It is one thing to explain that mortality in general is good for people in general. It is something else again to try to tell someone who has lost a parent, a wife, or a child that death is good. We don't dare try to do that. It would be cruel and thoughtless. All we can say to someone at a time like that is that vulnerability to death is one of the given conditions of life. We can't explain it any more than we can explain life itself. We can't control it, or sometimes even postpone it. All we can do is try to rise beyond the question 'Why did it happen?' and begin to ask the question 'What do I do now that it has happened?'*

Rabbi Kushner's question leads us to ask another: why would God, if God is all-powerful, all-loving, all-knowing, allow bad things to happen to good people? As the Greek philosopher Epicurus (later echoed by David Hume) declared: either God is cruel and uncaring or God is not all-powerful and all-knowing. Where do we go from here?

My studies have led me to the tentative answer put forward by Process Theology: the idea that God is not complete but still developing along with us and so is neither all-good, all-knowing, nor all-powerful. Where does this leave hope?

Carole Grace, a member of Kensington Unitarians and a psychotherapist, gave me an answer when she wrote about her experience of working in Cambodia during the Vietnam War. There were days, she wrote, when 'my faith in anything evaporated'. She found hope in the impression made on her by two children. A girl of six, who had lost limbs, was 'psychologically strong'. The boy of around eight suffered even more because of the effects of napalm-inflicted scars and burns. Carole writes that the boy was withdrawn, probably not only because of the physical pain, but the shudders of those who saw him. Yet the girl chatted and smiled at him and kept him company. Carole saw that, while he found it hard to respond, there was 'real communication between them, and the girl managed to convey love'. Hope remained because, as Carole concluded, 'Although they had both suffered … they kept their humanity and looked after each other lovingly'.

Group discussion (10 minutes)

☐ Invite brief responses to the reading before seeking responses to the following question:

- *The problem of evil and suffering is one of the strongest arguments used against the existence of God. But is it that simple? This first reading invites us to reflect on why bad things happen to good people. It moves us to ask what we do in the face of what has happened, and where is the hope. Reflecting on your own experience of life's darker moments, how does this reading invite you to respond to the questions that it asks?*

Break/music (15 minutes)

Time for a pause from the words and an opportunity for a comfort break.

Reading 2: *Reflection on the Power of Good* by Kate Dean

The suffering in the world often challenges the notion of a benevolent deity.
Perhaps God is a process rather than a being?
In these modern times, when we are exposed to so much information,
scientific explanation, and mistrust of religious institutions,
is there a place for God, or 'goodness'?

The Unitarian peace campaigner and humanist, Richenda Barbour, used to say 'I believe in a God with two Os'.
If we can see God as the sum of all the good things in the world, we can affect the spirit of God by cultivating our love and compassion.
When we look within, we connect with a divine compass, a guide to walking the uncertain path that lies before us.

Let us honour and sustain the 'God of our hearts', the divine that dwells within, so that we may become a blessing in the world.

Activity (10 minutes) and small-group sharing (25 minutes)

☐ Activity: Invite participants to do some free-writing, beginning with the phrase 'I believe in a God with two Os ...'. They should write without thinking too much, just letting the words flow on to the page.

☐ Ask the participants in small groups of three or four to share their responses to the act of free-writing, or just say something about their experience of it.

Small-group responses shared with the larger group (5 minutes)

Gather the full group together and invite members to share with each other a few of the common points (or any differences) that they found in their small groups.

Announcements

☐ Confirm the date and time of the next meeting.

☐ Explain any activity for participants to engage with at home before Week 4.

☐ Remind them to bring a notebook and their copy of this book next week.

☐ Other housekeeping information.

☐ Invite any questions for clarification.

Check-out (10 minutes)

☐ Invite participants to share a word or phrase about how they are feeling, or what they are taking away from the session.

Closing Words

For our closing words this evening we have chosen these words by Albert Schweitzer, the humanitarian, philosopher, and gifted musician:

At times our own light goes out and is rekindled by a spark from another person. Each of us has cause to think with deep gratitude of those who have lit the flame within us.

Week 4: The big questions

Part 2: The cycle of life: birth, death, and everything in between

Preparation for facilitators

You will need:

- Any music that you intend to play, and the means with which to play it.

- A box of tissues.

- A large copy of the Group Covenant Summary from Appendix (i) on display (optional).

- Spare paper and pens for any participants who haven't brought a notebook.

Chalice-candle lighting and silence (3 minutes)

☐ If the group is meeting in person, arrange chairs in a circle. If it's an online meeting, choose the 'gallery view' option so that all the participants fit on one screen. You might wish to play some meditative music in the background.

☐ Light the chalice candle when all are gathered (or invite a member of the group to do so).

☐ Then fade the music and invite them to share a time of stillness.

Opening Words by Michael Allured

Life is one huge tapestry: a blanket of multiple and multi-coloured knitted squares sewn together. It's the joy of belonging and loving, the heartbreak of losing, and everything in between – even the domestic chores – that creates the whole of our lives. All the seemingly small and insignificant things are part of our spiritual journey too. May we embrace them, honour them, nurture them. They too are part of our days. They too yield life lessons. May we embrace the cycle of life within the circle of the years and glimpse life's purpose anew.

Check-in (15 minutes)

☐ Welcome everyone to Week 4 of *Soul Deep* gatherings.

☐ Invite participants to respond to the question 'How is your heart?'

Overview of session (2 minutes)

☐ Remind everyone about the group agreement and ways of working together, especially *personal (not general) sharing … confidentiality … * and *deep listening.*

☐ Introduce Week 4 as an invitation to explore the grand sweep of life's cycle: birth, death, and everything in between – life's joys and sorrows, and how they shape us.

☐ Remind the group of the format for the session if necessary.

Reading 1: *Life is Always Becoming* by Yvonne Aburrow

Both Taoism and Paganism emphasise the dynamic balance in Nature between growth and decay, darkness and light, yin and yang, male and female, expansion and contraction. Balance is not just a steady-state, but a dynamic equilibrium. New birth is balanced by death; growth is balanced by decay; light and activity are balanced by darkness and rest. If everything grew and expanded all the time, there would eventually be no space in the world for new growth: the old growth would block out the light. So death and decay and darkness are not evil, but necessary components of the natural processes of life and change.

The darkness is necessary for rest, growth, and regeneration. Death is not evil, but a necessary adjunct to life. If there was no death and dissolution, there could be no change or growth. The cycle of birth, life, death, and rebirth is part of the dance. Suffering is also part of the process of growth; just as a tree is shaped by the wind, we are shaped by our experiences. It is only by experiencing suffering that we acquire sufficient depth to know the fullness of joy. It is then that the full light of consciousness dawns in us, and we achieve mystical communion with the divine.

But we cannot connect with the divine by stressing about it, but rather by relaxing and finding the inner stillness and space that is already there. All we have to do is to remember who we really are; to reconnect with the ebb and flow of the cycles of life. Everything is cyclical – the seasons, the tides, the orbits of the planets – why not human life? But it is not just a ceaseless round of the same old things, repeated ad nauseam. Everything changes; everything is always becoming something else; nothing is ever lost.

Group discussion (10 minutes)

☐ Yvonne Aburrow has written: *'Death and decay and darkness are not evil, but necessary components of the natural processes of life and change ... It is only by experiencing suffering that we acquire sufficient depth to know the fullness of joy...'.* What do you understand by the ideas in this reading? How does it align with your approach to life?

Break/music (15 minutes)

Time for a pause from the words and an opportunity for a comfort break.

Reading 2: *How Contemplating Death Can Help Us Live Life More Fully* by Kate Dean

As a Unitarian minister serving an open-minded spiritual community, I encounter discussions about death regularly. Families who are adrift having lost a loved one agonise over planning a funeral which would honour the wishes of the deceased. The most successful memorial services combine suggestions made by the departed person before their death with suggestions from the family; a completely pre-planned service gives no room for manoeuvre, but if the loved one has not talked at all about what they want, that can cause even more distress to their family.

This is why I wanted to ensure that there was a safe space in my neighbourhood where people could talk about death. We hold monthly Death Cafés, following a model created in the secular world by Jon Underwood. At a Death Café, people, often strangers to each other, gather to eat cake, drink tea, and discuss death. The objective is 'to increase awareness of death with a view to helping people make the most of their (finite) lives'. A Death Café

(in Christian faith settings sometimes called a Compassion Café) is a group-directed discussion of death with no agenda, objectives, or themes. We have made adjustments to the model which include dividing into smaller groups of six people where everyone has five minutes of uninterrupted time to say what is on their mind concerning the subject. We find that, despite beginning as strangers, people connect at a very deep level and often leave the session as friends.

One participant declared: 'It is beautiful how vulnerable some people are and courageous to share this vulnerability and doubt about the death issue.'

Facing the ultimate questions about the end of life as part of the cycle of life can help us appreciate what we have, come to terms with loss, and recommit to living life more fully.

Activity (10 minutes) and small-group sharing (25 minutes)

☐ Invite members of the group to respond to these suggestions:

☐ List six words which arise when you think about the cyclical nature of life.

☐ Look at the words. Do you see any connections? Are any of the words a surprise to you?

☐ Describe (in writing, or later in the small-group sharing) any ways in which you have celebrated or honoured a transition in your life.

☐ In small groups of three or four, share your responses to the activity, or just say something about your experience of it.

Small-group responses shared with the larger group (5 minutes)

☐ Gather the full group together. Invite members to share with each other a few of the common points or differences that they found in their small groups.

Announcements

☐ Confirm the date and time of the next meeting.

☐ Explain any activity for participants to engage with at home before Week 5.

☐ Remind participants to bring a notebook and their copy of this book next week.

☐ Other housekeeping information.

☐ Invite any questions for clarification.

Check-out (10 minutes)

☐ Invite participants to share a word or phrase about how they are feeling, or what they are taking away from the session.

Closing words: *A Winter Prayer – Anticipating Spring* by Jeffrey Bowes

When we think of the turn of the season which we expect to happen soon, we know that, whatever the coming months may bring, we may have great hope for the future.

In all the years we each have lived, the spring has faithfully followed the gloomiest of winters.
From that faithfulness we learn to have hope.
Hope for ourselves;
no matter how chill we may feel the winters to be,
no matter how hard our lives may be,
no matter how dispirited we may become,
we can and we do come to a springtime of light and love
and life and growth.

Because we have hope for ourselves, we may have hope for others;
for our family and friends – sometimes relationships can seem chilly and distant.

For our neighbours and acquaintances, colleagues, and fellow workers –
sometimes our attempts to understand and move
towards another can fail and make us feel as though ice-bound.
For the people of other lands – sometimes relations between states can seem icy cold,
sometimes the peoples can suffer hardship such as we might
if our frozen farmlands never thawed.

Our hope for others is that, in trying to reflect and share the warmth of the love we see and feel in the faithful return of the spring, we can help to thaw the ice of difficult relationships, to ease the hardship caused by the delay of the growing season.

We know that the damp and mists of the coming months will be signs that the earth is warming once again.

As our world turns toward the sun, as the days lengthen and fresh, green, growth begins, so we can see that even through tears and sorrows we can turn, in our hearts and minds, towards that which is light and life in all we have. We too can turn, and be warmed.

Week 5: What gets in the way?

Part 1: Spiritual baggage and how perceptions of God can be barriers on our spiritual journey

Preparation for facilitators

You will need:

- Any music that you intend to play, and the means with which to play it.

- A box of tissues.

- A large copy of the Group Covenant Summary from Appendix (i) on display (optional)

- Spare paper and pens for any participants who haven't brought a notebook.

Chalice-candle lighting and silence (3 minutes)

☐ If the group is meeting in person, arrange chairs in a circle. If it's an online meeting, choose the 'gallery view' option so that all the participants fit on one screen. You might wish to play some meditative music in the background.

☐ Light the chalice candle when all are gathered – or invite a member of the group to light it.

☐ Then fade the music and invite them into a time of stillness.

Opening words by Kate Dean

Our bags are packed, we are ready for a spiritual adventure,
But something holds us back.
We question ourselves: are we on the right path?
The old skeletons clank in the closet,
the past hurts and slights emerge,
and perhaps there are even wounds
from a more restricted belief system.

The poet Amanda Gorman wrote:
'For there is always light,
if only we're brave enough to see it.
If only we're brave enough to be it'.[3]

If we are brave enough to be it for each other,
there is always light,
and that will lead us on our way.

Check-in (15 minutes)

☐ Welcome everyone to Week 5 of *Soul Deep* gatherings.

☐ Invite participants to respond to the question 'How is your heart?'

Overview of session (2 minutes)

☐ Remind everyone about the group agreement and ways of working together, especially *personal (not general) sharing ... confidentiality ... and deep listening.*

---

3   Words taken from the poem 'The Hill We Climb', which Gorman recited at the inauguration of Joe Biden as US President in 2021. We also recommend reading the full poem!

☐ Introduce Week 5 as an invitation to explore the grand sweep of life's cycle: birth, death, and everything in between; life's joys and sorrows, and how they shape us.

☐ Draw the group's attention to the format, pointing out that for this session the activity and small-group sharing will happen after the first reading (and not the second reading, as in previous weeks).

Reading 1: *Bear's Blue Backpack* by Kate Dean

This is a story about a bear. Bear set out on a journey to The Great Tree, hoping to find The Answer. Bear had a favourite blue backpack, and in it was packed everything needed for the journey, including memories – both good and bad – plus love from friends, and a fear of spiders.

Along the way Bear had all kinds of adventures and met all kinds of different creatures. After many days of travel, Bear got to The Great Tree, with a very heavy backpack filled with all the things that had been collected along the way.

Bear addressed the tree: 'Oh Great Tree, I have travelled many miles, I have journeyed for hours and days. Please will you tell me The Answer?'

Bear then bowed low and waited. The Great Tree simply responded, 'Look in your blue backpack'.

Bear looked inside and found a floppy sun hat and a tin of baked beans. 'Look in your blue backpack!' the voice spoke again. Bear looked further and found a fear of spiders.

'Look in your blue backpack!' Right at the bottom Bear found all those happy memories and bundles of love from friends and family. *'This must be the answer!'* thought Bear.

> So Bear went home, and along the way decided to donate the
> food to Squirrel's food bank, and the hat and other items to
> Hedgehog's charity shop, then headed home to the warmth of
> loved ones, feeling lighter with every step.

Activity (15 minutes) and small-group sharing (25 minutes)

Guided visualisation – Travels With My Backpack

☐ Offer the following meditation to participants, allowing for short
pauses after each sentence.

Begin by sitting comfortably, with nothing in your hands, and close
your eyes if you wish. ...

Lace your fingers together with your thumbs touching, creating a
circle of energy throughout your body. ... Put your hands in your lap,
resting near your belly button. ... Breathe deeply, using your stomach
rather than your chest. ... Focus on the flow of air and energy as you
breathe in and out. ... Imagine yourself walking along a path lined
with beautiful trees and plants. ...

You are carrying a backpack. ... Your spiritual backpack weighs heavy
on your back. ... Imagine it, filled with all your precious memories
and experiences as well as some sustenance for the journey: those
experiences that have made you the person you are today ... those
painful moments, as well as joyful moments. ... After a long journey,
you decide to take a rest. ...You find a welcoming tree, swaying in the
warm breeze. Sit under the tree. ...

Open up your backpack and look inside. ... You notice all your treasure,
those symbols of your memories and experiences, good and bad. ...

Pull out two objects and look at them carefully. ... Consider what they mean to you. ... How do they relate to the baggage that you need to release, or traits in yourself that you treasure? ... [pause] Slowly open your eyes and return to the circle.

Activity

☐ Take 10 minutes to think, draw, or write about your experience, considering the question: *how do the treasured objects from your backpack relate to the baggage that you need to release, or traits in yourself that you treasure?*

☐ In small groups of three or four, share your responses to the activity or just say something about your baggage, or about the experience more generally.

Small-group responses shared with the larger group (5 minutes)

☐ Gather the full group together and invite people to share a few of the common points or differences that they found in their small groups.

Break/music (15 minutes)

Time for a pause from the words and an opportunity for a comfort break.

Reading 2: *Religious Baggage* by Michael Allured

Rabbi Lionel Blue once observed that religion can make you very nice or very nasty, but that he thought it had made him nicer than he would have been without it. Even a few atheists are likely to have enjoyed a friendly debate with the famously gay radio rabbi, because he saw God as a friend with whom you could have a cosy chat, or get annoyed with – and who wouldn't get annoyed by being shouted at. But there are many perceptions of God: some helpful and others positively destructive and downright dangerous.

Each religion has its own name or names for God. How we think about God, Lord, YHWH, the Divine, Allah, Jehovah, or Brahman depends on so many factors: the culture and era in which we are born, our parents' and family faith (or lack of it), the type of education that we receive, and our own life experiences. Before the age of science, people believed in a God who kept order; they did so in order to explain the inexplicable and to offer hope of a better life in the next world, because this one was so unbearable. Organised religion, particularly if it is linked to the State, is often about power and control.

Understandably some people challenge institutionalised religion for the damage that it has done to individuals, and even to nations. All that talk about sin, all that bowing down, all that punishment is either embraced or rejected. I was about 13 or 14 when, because I am gay, I was told by a fellow pupil that I disgusted God. That was probably a fairly common perception in the 1970s. It didn't ring true for me then, and it doesn't now. It makes me sad that anyone could think that God cares about such things when there is so much suffering in the world to worry about.

The hymn 'Leave behind your bags and baggage' offers a kinder perception in the lines 'Let the God of all our mercies breathe around you everywhere'.[4] I prefer this image of God and the friendly and sympathetic Being embodied in advice that Lionel Blue passes on to us from a sage: if you were planting a tree and were told the Messiah was coming, you'd finish planting the tree and only then go out to welcome him.

Group discussion (10 minutes)

☐ Invite brief reactions to the readings before inviting responses to these questions:

- What object in your backpack do you feel you need to leave behind, so that you can be free to become your authentic self? You may find it helpful to think about what ideas and practices continue to stifle you, and then reflect on what brings you a feeling of peace and well-being.

- Take another look in your backpack. What special object, quality, or person's photograph have you kept to help you come alive, and why?

Announcements

☐ Confirm the date and time of the next meeting.

☐ Explain any activity for participants to engage with at home before Week 6.

☐ Remind participants to bring a notebook and their copy of this book next week.

4   Peter Samson, 'Leave behind your bags and baggage', Hymn 87, *Sing Your Faith*.

☐ Other housekeeping information.

☐ Invite any questions for clarification.

Check-out (10 minutes)

☐ Invite participants to share a word or phrase about how they are feeling, or what they are taking away from the session.

Closing words: *Tao* by Michael Allured

Close no doors to Tao[5] to undo your translucent seeing.

Live through the questions

into an even deeper known unknown.

Seek solitude, honouring your time to sit with the discombobulation you find.

Sacred texts abound, and God is unknowable,

recognisable only in the perfections and imperfections of us all.

Close no doors to more seeking of yet unknown answers.

Meanwhile be the good in the world that feeds your soul.

---

5   Tao is a Chinese concept of the basis for things to exist and events to happen.

Week 6: What gets in the way?

Part 2: Pressures of everyday life (time, finance, health, work–life balance)

Preparation for facilitators

You will need:

- Any music that you intend to play, and the means with which to play it.

- A box of tissues.

- A large copy of the Group Covenant Summary from Appendix (i) on display (optional).

- Spare paper and pens for any participants who have not brought a notebook.

- Every participant will need a piece of paper, scissors, and a pen for the activity.

Chalice-candle lighting and silence (3 minutes)

☐ If the group is meeting in person, arrange chairs in a circle. If it's an online meeting, choose the 'gallery view' option so that all the participants fit on one screen. You might wish to play some meditative music in the background.

☐ When everyone is gathered, light the chalice candle, or invite a member of the group to do so.

☐ Then fade the music and invite everyone into a time of stillness.

Opening words: *'It's complicated'* by Jane Blackall

In the days, and weeks, and months to come – whatever they may bring – let us remember: *'It's complicated'*. And not shy away from that reality, but instead face it, courageously, together. And as we do our best to discern the way ahead, individually and collectively, let us remind each other of our guiding Unitarian principles: affirming the inherent worth and dignity of every person, and the interdependence of all, let us make our decisions with human well-being and flourishing in mind. Let us be particularly mindful of our responsibility to those who are disadvantaged and suffering. And let us always keep before us the vision of a better world, for the greater good of all.

Check-in (15 minutes)

☐ Welcome everyone to Week 6 of *Soul Deep* gatherings.

☐ Invite participants to respond to the question 'How is your heart?'

Overview of session (5 minutes)

☐ Remind everyone about the group agreement and ways of working together, especially *personal (not general) sharing ... confidentiality ... and deep listening.*

☐ Introduce Week 6 as an invitation to reflect on what are the blocks to enriching our spirituality and connection with others, and how we might move beyond these factors that get in the way.

☐ Explain that the format returns to the usual pattern of engaging in the activity and the small-group sharing after the second reading.

Reading 1: *Work and Play* by Kate Dean

I was standing by a construction site recently (as you do when you have a toddler), observing the conveyor belt which moved a load of soil and rubble up over a wall so that it fell into a skip on the street. I reflected on my industrial design training, noticing, for the first time, the cleats on the sloping conveyor belt which helped it transport the soil without it falling off on the way. I observed the construction worker who monitored the flow, levelling off the soil with a spade every so often to ensure that the skip was filled evenly. We stood there for some time, my son and I – what did the worker think about us staring at him as he worked? This sort of behaviour seems to be quite acceptable when you have a small boy in tow or, rather, a small boy leading the way to watch the machines. In the scene, I was aware of the contrast between my past and possible career paths and my present practice of mindfulness and my need to let my mind rest. In this scene, with us two standing in the sunshine watching the day go by, were work and play, learning and resting, pause and activity – perhaps even the makings of a beautiful life.

Much is spoken about getting the work/life balance right, but if our work in this world is right for us, it is no longer a choice between work and life, but a commitment to honour our whole divine selves through the work we do and the play we enjoy. In many ways, work gives meaning and purpose to our lives, and play gives us rest and joy. And we need both in order to be fulfilled and happy.

> We Unitarians are more interested in the here and now than in the hereafter, so I think we need to make *now* count. We have a responsibility to make the most of our time here as a celebration of life and through the worship of that which we call divine.

Group discussion (10 minutes)

☐ Encourage brief responses to the reading before inviting responses to these questions:

- What aspects of your life seem unbalanced at the moment?

- In what ways can you, or do you, incorporate spiritual practices into your daily life?

Break/music (15 minutes)

Time for a pause from the words and an opportunity for a comfort break.

Reading 2: *Spiritual Journeys Can Feel Stuck* by Michael Allured

We sometimes feel stuck. There is simply too much noise and traffic in everyday life. The jigsaw pieces of life are scattered. The physicality of living in bodies forces on us practicalities that crowd our spirits, and we are left feeling that there is so little time to cultivate the gardens of our souls. Perhaps one of the few ways open to us is to learn to use the moments in between all of the stuff that we see as getting in the way. Here are just some of the things that can stifle our spirits:

- physical illness and chronic pain

- the instability inherent in the living of our lives that causes us to worry about where we live, the resources we have to live on, the safety of those we love

---

- world events over which we have no control

- a depression that we don't fully understand and can't explain

- the mind games that we are drawn into, either of our own or other people's making, creating real or imagined situations, leading us down insecure roads and towards a denial of who we truly are.

How to tend to souls in this seeming chaos? I hear a voice whispering 'go with the flow' in uncharted waters. If we acknowledge that we are spirit or soul as well as mind and body, the way to peace and fulfilment is surely to learn how we can bend more easily when the wind blows?

I do not know how possible it is to embrace the advice of the Sufi poet Rumi to invite in the unwelcome guests even if they bring a crowd of sorrows that sweep your home of its furniture. Yet these unwelcome guests (you will have your own) are, sadly, our reality. How can we make the best of them and still make those beautiful sounds of the soul that nourish us and each other? Here are some tentative answers:

- Find bright stars to help steer your course.

- Cultivate the practice of treating unanswered questions as friends (or at least acquaintances).

- Go on a journey of self-discovery to find the fulcrum[6] that supports and sustains you.

- Try to live in the moment and know that your small steps are enough.

---

6   Fulcrum: the point at which a lever is placed to get purchase, or on which it turns or is supported; a thing that plays an essential role in an activity or situation.

Activity (15 minutes) and small-group sharing (25 minutes)

Piecing together our lives

The 19th-century Transcendentalist Henry David Thoreau spent two years in deep contemplation in a wooden cabin by Walden Pond in Massachusetts. He wrote, 'I went to the woods because I wished to live deliberately, to front only the essential facts of life, and see if I could not learn what it had to teach, and not, when I came to die, discover that I had not lived. I did not wish to live what was not life; living is so dear.'

When we find it difficult to 'go with the flow', it's useful to return to the parts of ourselves which cause us discomfort and see if we can create pictures with the jigsaw pieces of our lives.

☐ Preparation: give each participant a piece of paper, scissors, and a pen.

☐ Invite each participant to draw wavy lines on the paper to create 8 pieces (see diagram). Cut the paper roughly along the lines and shuffle the pieces.

☐ Invite them each to write on separate puzzle pieces 4 words or phrases to describe 4 pressures in their life right now.

☐ Then invite them to write on separate puzzle pieces 4 words or phrases to describe 4 strengths or sources of support that they have.

☐ They should then spend some time carefully putting their puzzles back together and notice any connections between the different pieces.

☐ Invite them to make notes, meditate, or draw diagrams to illustrate any insights that they have discovered.

☐ Suggest that they share the results in pairs in order to engage in reflection at a deeper level: what insights did they gain?

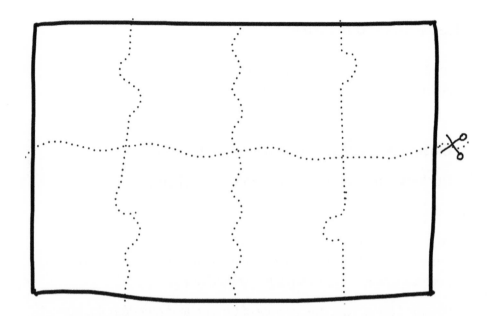

Small-group responses shared with the larger group (5 minutes)

☐ Gather the full group together. Invite them to share with each other a few of the common points or differences that they found in their small groups.

Announcements

☐ Confirm the date and time of the next meeting.

☐ Explain any activity for participants to engage with at home before Week 7.

☐ Remind participants to bring a notebook and their copy of this book next week.

☐ Other housekeeping information.

☐ Invite any questions for clarification.

Check-out (10 minutes)

☐ Invite participants to share a word or phrase about how they are feeling, or what they are taking away from the session.

Closing words: *Greater Equilibrium* by Kate Dean

Our lives consist of connections and interruptions.

Each interaction creates a new piece of ourselves.

We strive to find the right balance of time spent with loved ones, time spent on satisfying work, rest and relaxation, and all those necessary tasks which keep a household going.

We don't always get the balance of tension and release right, but we can commit to taking time to observe our actions and taking small steps towards a greater equilibrium.

Week 7: Finding ways to deepen our soul connections

Preparation for facilitators

You will need:

- Any music that you intend to play, and the means with which l to play it.

- A box of tissues.

- A large copy of the Group Covenant Summary from Appendix (i) on display (optional).

- Spare paper and pens for any participants who haven't brought a notebook.

Chalice-candle lighting and silence (3 minutes)

☐ If the group is meeting in person, arrange chairs in a circle. If it's an online meeting, choose the 'gallery view' option so that all the participants fit on one screen. You might wish to play some meditative music in the background.

☐ When all are gathered, light the chalice candle or invite a member of the group to do so.

☐ Then fade the music and invite them into a time of stillness.

Opening words: *Love and Courage* by Linda Hart

Living with love and courage is what I hope we do in community, ever and always.

Ministry means to seek to create transformative community.

We say:
  we are on the road,
  we are trying
  to make that world we dream,
  release the prisoners, feed the hungry,
  clothe the naked,
  lift up those who mourn,
  we are trying to make it better.

We say:
  we strive,
  we have failed to be what we meant,
  do what we meant,
  failed to live what we hoped.

We say:
  the world gets dark,
  and we get lost,

And we say:
  here's my hand,
  we'll find the way together.

And we say:
  this way can be hard,
  but look – there are tiny buds
  on that tree,
  look – there's the sunrise.

Check-in (15 minutes)

☐ Welcome everyone to Week 7 of *Soul Deep* gatherings.

☐ Invite participants to respond to the question 'How is your heart?'

Overview of session

☐ Remind everyone about the group agreement and ways of working together, especially *personal (not general) sharing ... confidentiality ... and deep listening.*

☐ Introduce Week 7 by acknowledging that doing soul work is hard and takes discipline and commitment. This week is all about how we can find ways to deepen a commitment to do this work, on our own and as part of a Unitarian community.

Reading 1: *Blessing the World* by Kate Dean

The spiritual teacher Rachel Naomi Remen said 'When we bless others, we offer them refuge from an indifferent world.'

Blessing the world is an act of recognising the interconnectedness that binds us all. In a society often consumed by individualism and materialism, the act of blessing becomes a profound acknowledgment: 'I see you. I hear you. You are not alone.' As the pendulum swings between self-reliance and communal bonds, maintaining our spiritual communities becomes ever more important.

> In positive psychology, there is a practice of accepting adversity while focusing on the positive impact that we can make. This is inspiring, but it is not new. The Stoic philosophers of the Roman Empire also reflected this wisdom. The Emperor and philosopher Marcus Aurelius wrote: 'You have power over your mind – not over outside events. Realise this, and you will find strength.'
>
> The Roman poet Horace was influenced by the Stoics, and his most famous message calls us to 'seize the day'. Aurelius urged '... your time has a limit set to it. Use it, then, to advance your enlightenment; or it will be gone, and never in your power again.'
>
> *Carpe diem*, Horace might have replied: *seize the day.*

Group discussion (10 minutes)

☐ Encourage brief responses to the reading before inviting answers to these questions:

- If you have been part of a spiritual community, how has the experience affected the way you live your life?

- In what ways can you become a 'blessing to the world' through contributing to the well-being of others?

Break/music (15 minutes)

Time for a pause from the words and an opportunity for a comfort break.

Reading 2: *On Humility* by Celia Cartwright

In our Unitarian congregations, we strive to welcome diversity, a diversity of religious or spiritual understanding, and a diversity of people. We strive to make all welcome. But sometimes we find ourselves judging others because they upset our expectations of what is 'normal'. Humility requires of us that we recognise our own resistance to acceptance, and open ourselves to the reality that all God's children are not the same, and that's OK. Humility asks that if we want to become the faith we pledge ourselves to hold, we must not judge and deny, learning only from our in-built prejudices. Rather, we should recognise when we lean into judgement. When we accept that with compassion, knowledge, and the humility to know we don't know everything, then we will grow with knowing. And by the same token, we must offer ourselves the same gifts, and not judge those things that we feel we should not be, think, fear, or feel. Instead, let us explore their meaning, with humility and gentleness.

When I first realised what humility was, in practice, in my daily life, I realised I didn't have to pretend to be more than I am any more. And with that came the freedom to become more than I had been, to let go my fears of being an imposter in my own life. I remember sharing life histories with a friend. Mine was a highlighted version featuring the bad stuff, with cameos for the good stuff. My friend was quiet for a while, and then said, 'Do you realise that at every stage when you reached the darkest of places, there was someone who called you back, gave you a way out?' I hadn't realised, but she was right. Running through those moments, every time I could have given up, an angel appeared and with very little hoo-ha led me on to a different path. Not always right away, but at some point, someone helped me. 'And', she said, 'you also had to let them in to help.' Now there's a lesson in humility that I cannot ever forget.

Activity (10 minutes) and small-group sharing (25 minutes)

Writing a prayer or meditation

Our approach to prayer or meditation relates to our concept of the divine. Some find connection through nature, others through musical expression. Many of us will know the profound experience of listening to or performing a particular piece of music. Whether it is something familiar and beloved, or something new and exciting, it finds a connection with the soul and lifts our spirits and can be a kind of prayer.

One might question whether it is worth praying, whether God would take any notice. As Unitarians, we are free to make up our own minds on this one, but the liberal Jewish rabbi John Rayner suggests: 'Even if prayer cannot, in any straightforward sense, influence God, it can certainly influence man [or the person praying]. It opens up a channel through which God's power, always available to those who seek it, can flow into the mind of the worshipper. Therefore, if he prays for a spiritual quality (such as courage), the effect may very well be an increase of that quality.'

Rabbi Marc Gellman suggests that there are four kinds of prayer: *'Please! Thanks! Oops!* and *Wow!'* Or in holy-speak: *Supplication*: pleading for ourselves ('petition') or on behalf of others ('intercession') ... *Thanksgiving* ... *Confession* ... and *Adoration*.

☐ Invite participants to write a prayer or poetic meditation using one or more of Rabbi Gellman's focal points: *Please! Thanks! Oops!* or *Wow!*

☐ Small-group sharing: in groups of three or four, share your prayers or say something about your experience of trying to write a prayer or meditation.

Small-group responses shared with the larger group (5 minutes)

☐ Gather the full group together. Invite participants to share with each other a few of the common points or differences that they found in their small groups.

Announcements

☐ Confirm the date and time of the next meeting.

☐ Explain any activity for participants to engage with at home before Week 8.

☐ If the group wants a more self-directed approach to their final week, they can co-create a closing ritual, using the instructions in Appendix (iii): *Week 8 Closing Ritual.*

☐ Remind participants to bring a notebook and their copy of this book next week.

☐ Ask whether the group is interested in continuing in some form after Week 8. If so, point them to the section on continuing the journey (pages 82–84), which could be discussed next week. If participants have made suggestions of other readings and resources, they should make a note of them so that all suggestions can be compiled as material for future sessions.

☐ Announce other housekeeping information, and what the group will be doing in Week 8 to honour the time that they have spent together, and what they have shared and appreciated about each other.

☐ Invite any questions for clarification.

Check-out (10 minutes)

☐ Invite participants to share a word or phrase about how they are feeling, or what they are taking away from the session.

Closing words

The vital work of the spirit calls us to open our hearts and minds. So let us ponder our truth and seek to find the courage to speak it – and the love to live it. It begins with love.

Week 8: Wrap-up. Gathering and bringing in the harvest

Preparation for facilitators

You will need:

- Any music that you intend to play, and the means with which to play it.

- A box of tissues.

- Materials for Farewell Memory Messages: good-quality A4 paper or card, colourful pens/pencils, and stickers or other decorations, if you wish.

- Materials for the Common Bowl Ritual activity: a copy of the list of quotations on pages 76–81, cut into separate strips, and a bowl to place them in.

Chalice-candle lighting and silence (3 minutes)

☐ If the group is meeting in person, arrange chairs in a circle. If it's an online meeting, choose the 'gallery view' option so that all the participants fit on one screen. You might wish to play some meditative music in the background.

☐ When the participants are gathered, light the chalice candle – or invite a member of the group to light it.

☐ Then fade the music and invite everyone into a time of stillness.

Opening words: *We Gather As Pilgrims* ... by Michael Allured

We have gathered as pilgrims, each on our own journey, and together on a shared adventure. We still do not fully know what is in the heart of another: the pain, the fear, the sorrow, the elation, the joy, the meaning, the peace. All there is to do is continue our listening.

And so we gather together as a unique group of souls for a final time on this stage of our spiritual journey to renew our heart connections. Together we have shared, explored, discovered through silence and story. In our quiet listening to and receiving what is offered, we have given and received our emerging insights.

In our remaining time together may we again hold a shared and safe space for each other: a space for listening with open hearts, a space for finding meaning in our sharing, a space for feeling gratitude.

Check-in (15 minutes)

☐ Welcome everyone to Week 8 of *Soul Deep* gatherings.

☐ Invite participants to respond to the question 'How is your heart?'

Overview of session (2 minutes)

☐ Remind everyone about the group agreement and ways of working together, especially *personal (not general) sharing ... confidentiality ... and deep listening.*

☐ Introduce Week 8 as being about gathering in the harvest of all the group's sharing and reflection over the previous seven weeks together.

☐ Explain that there is a reading with questions to help everyone reflect on the whole course, followed by two group activities. The first activity is an opportunity for members to write memory messages to each other. The second activity is a closing ritual using a collection of quotations from what we call 'the Common Bowl'.[7]

☐ Note: if the group has chosen to co-create a closing ritual, this would replace the two activities above.

☐ Read out the titles of each weekly session, to remind the group of the themes that have been covered in the course. You may choose to divide this task among the participants.

Reading 1: *How We Spend Our Days* by Jane Blackall

Whether we are striving to make a particularly big splash in the world or not, we will all leave a legacy of some sort when our time is up, and what it amounts to will emerge out of how we have chosen to spend our days. Making our lives meaningful is not primarily about striving for newsworthy achievements and worldly status though. Think, instead, about the legacy of love and caring you might leave – by raising a family, helping to organise a community, standing up for people who are downtrodden and discriminated against, tending a little plot of land – you might not win a Nobel Prize in the process, but it will still add up to a life very well spent.

---

7   The term 'Common Bowl' is used in two volumes of *Evensong* gatherings by Barbara Hamilton-Holway, published by Skinner House Books.

Group discussion and 'check-out' through closing reflections (20 minutes)

☐ Questions to prompt discussion:

- How do the ideas in this reading resonate with your own life experience? You may wish to reflect on significant events, your passions and interests, achievements (large or small), and relationships.

- Looking back to Week 1, how has your spirituality been nourished or strengthened by being part of this group during our time together (16 hours)?

Activity: *Farewell Memory Messages* (20 minutes)

☐ You will need sheets of good-quality A4 paper (if possible of different colours) and pens/pencils, maybe stickers or other decorations if you wish.

☐ Give everyone a sheet of paper and a pen.

☐ Ask them to write their name (quite small) in the centre, with plenty of space around the outside for people to write messages.

☐ Ask them to write 'Farewell' in a size that is readable to them at the top of the page.

☐ Ask them to pass the paper to the person on their left in the circle and for each person to write a short 'message of hope and encouragement', or draw a picture on the page in front of them, addressed to the person whose name is written in the centre.

☐ Note that if there are group members who have a visual impairment you may want to remind everyone to write legibly. Check with the relevant group members how large they need the writing to be in order to read it comfortably.

☐ Keep the sheets moving to the left until everyone has written on each other's sheets. They can add drawings or other decorations if you wish.

☐ When the sheet comes back to its owner, **ask them not to read it immediately**.

☐ Then, when everyone has finished writing, ask them to look at their pages. (This can be quite moving for some people, so take your time with the reading.)

☐ Suggest that they keep the sheet to cheer themselves up if and when they are struggling with their spiritual journey after the course has ended, or if they simply wish to recall the experience of being together on this course.

Online adaptation

☐ If this is an online session, ask everyone to take time to write messages to each participant and then decide how to share them – whether doing so while everyone is together, by sending a direct message to each participant using the 'chat' function, or sending them to each participant afterwards.

Break/music (10 minutes)

Time for a pause from the words and an opportunity for a comfort break.

Activity: *Reflections from the Common Bowl closing ritual* (20 minutes)

☐ Preparation: Make a copy of the quotation pages below and cut them into separate strips so there are enough for at least one per participant.

☐ Place them in a bowl.

☐ Invite everyone to take a quotation.

☐ Begin with Opening Words: *When we are together in a circle of trust* by Michael Allured (see below).

☐ Then invite everyone to take turns to read their quotation, leaving a pause of three breaths between quotes.

☐ End with the Closing Words *Farewell Soul Deep* by Kate Dean.

Online adaptation

☐ If this is an online session, invite participants to choose a quotation at random, perhaps by closing their eyes and putting a finger on the page in the book to select a quote to read. Select the order of readers according to the method used by the group to 'go around the circle' in other sessions.

Closing ritual

Opening Words: *When we are together in a circle of trust* by Michael Allured

The days that make up our lives are full of experiences. Most are incidental or repetitive. Others make their mark of sadness or joy. Do we pay enough attention to each kind? If the longing of our soul is for connection and contentment, one path towards that is self-reflection. But as our spiritual journey occurs in relationship to each other, our self-discovery will be enriched by travelling the road together. If this is so, how should our belonging to a Unitarian/Universalist community that values and nurtures its heart-centred work help our own and each other's awakening?

To discover or rediscover our authentic free spirit is to find ways together for personal and shared contemplation of the mystery within and the mystery beyond. It is a lifetime's endeavour, this path towards a richer understanding of ourselves in relationship with the Universe and other minds, other hearts. We exist in relationship to others and the world, and yet we are alone. None of us will ever know what's going on inside the heads of fellow travellers. And yet have you noticed that when we are together in a circle of trust with others who offer their vulnerability by sharing their own life's tragic and tender moments you may find – as I have – that many of our experiences are not dissimilar? From these connections the bonds of empathy grow. It is in these moments that we make space for the other – for each other. How shall we spend our days?

Quotations

Hospitality to strangers is greater than reverence for the name of God.
(Hebrew proverb)[8]

. . . .

There is a delicious evening when the whole body is one sense and imbibes delight through every pore.
(Henry David Thoreau)[9]

. . . .

Let us worship with our eyes and ears and fingertips; let us love the world through heart and mind and body.
(Kenneth L Patton)[10]

. . . .

If you are already blessed with connection and closeness ... treasure it. Maintain it. Consider what you might do to nurture and deepen the web of relationships you already have. And if you're not so blessed in this regard ... then lament ... But think about reaching out too ... trying something new to connect and find closeness. As we return to our daily lives, each one of us can reflect on the part we might play to help create a less lonely society, through the choices that we make.
(Jane Blackall)[11]

. . . .

The theologians gather dust upon the shelves ... but the poets are stained with my fingers and blotted with my tears. I never seem so near the truth as when I care not what I think or believe.
(John Haynes Holmes)[12]

---

8   Letter to the Hebrews 13:12.
9   'Solitude', *On Walden Pond*, 1854.
10 Reading 437, *Singing the Living Tradition*, Unitarian Universalist Association, Boston: Beacon Press.
11 From a sermon.
12 In George N. Marshall, *Challenge of a Liberal Faith*, 3rd edition (Boston: Skinner House Books, 1991), pp. 134–5.

All shall be well, and all shall be well, and all manner of thing shall be well.
(Julian of Norwich)[13]

. . . .

Nothing is ever lost. The gathering of life experience is like the laying down of compost. The leaves of individual events fall on to the heap, fade, and decay, and are transformed into memories which feed our sense of identity, which gives rise to new experiences.
(Yvonne Aburrow)

. . . .

Change is constant in life; it is the one thing we can rely on. Some people find it difficult to embrace change; others enjoy it. Without change, there would be no growth, no seasons, no new life. There would also be no death, but just try to imagine what immortality would be like – a barren state of existence with no excitement.
(Yvonne Aburrow)

. . . .

The misery here is terrible; and yet, late at night when the day has slunk away into the depths behind me, I often walk with a spring in my step along the barbed wire. And then time and time again, it soars straight from my heart – I can't help it, that's just the way it is, like some elementary force – the feeling that life is glorious and magnificent, and that one day we shall be building a whole new world.
(Etty Hillesum)[14]

---

13   *Revelations of Divine Love.*
14   Frank Woodhouse, *Etty Hillesum: A Life Transformed* (London: Continuum International, 2009), p. 127.

But the effect of her being on those around her was incalculably diffusive: for the growing good of the world is partly dependent on unhistoric acts; and that things are not so ill with you and me as they might have been is half owing to the number who lived faithfully a hidden life, and rest in unvisited tombs.

(George Eliot)[15]

. . . .

Paul Tillich, the German Protestant theologian, defined faith as 'the ultimate orientation of a person's life'. Yet what I believe about God and faith isn't easy to explain in sound bites and could even appear rather vague, not least because it might be summed up as a work in progress, an evolving theology.

(Michael Allured)

. . . .

… what with God being unknowable and all that – whatever we might say about God is going to be a bit wrong. Or a lot wrong … Once you've said something, and then you've 'unsaid' it, this apophatic process requires you to 'unsay' the thing you've just 'unsaid' as well! And this goes on and on for ever … It's nothing like other modes of theological or philosophical reflection. And that's why it's often been associated with the mystics. Going through this process of 'unsaying' is somehow supposed to disrupt your everyday ways of thinking and have a transformative effect.

(Jane Blackall)[16]

. . . .

Sometimes we have failed to do our best by others, and sometimes we have failed to do our best by ourselves. By learning from – but not holding on to – our mistakes, let us relinquish the resentments of our own failures.

(Jo James)[17]

15   *Middlemarch*, 1872.
16   From a sermon.
17   From a sermon, *Blues for Michael*.

Finish each day and be done with it. You have done what you could. Some blunders and absurdities no doubt crept in; forget them as soon as you can. Tomorrow is a new day; begin it well and serenely and with too high a spirit to be encumbered with your old nonsense.
(Ralph Waldo Emerson)[18]

. . . .

It is a feature of our society that we are goal-oriented: we value results and judge a thing by its outcome. We have become almost completely dislocated from the Holy, the sacred, the Divine. Being unmeasurable allows the dominant left brain to conclude that Deity is non-existent. Invisible, the eternal immortal slips quietly from view … And it is why we harshly judge lives on their achievements.
(Jo James)[19]

. . . .

Do the thing you fear, and the death of fear is certain.
(Mark Twain)[20]

. . . .

Do not be too timid and squeamish about your actions. All life is an experiment. The more experiments you make, the better. What if you do fail and get fairly rolled in the dirt once or twice? Up again you shall never be so afraid of a tumble.
(Ralph Waldo Emerson)[21]

. . . .

The spiritual teacher Rachel Naomi Remen said that 'When we bless others, we offer them refuge from an indifferent world'.
(Kate Dean)

18   https://quoteinvestigator.com/2018/12/19/finish-day/
19   From a sermon, *Blues for Michael.*
20   https://philosiblog.com/2011/09/21/
21   https://www.goodreads.com/quotes/375347

A Jewish friend recently asked me, 'At the end of your life, how are you going to know if you've been a good Unitarian?' From his point of view, being a good Jew required adherence to certain practices and abstaining from others … When I was thinking of being a good Unitarian, the one word that came to mind was 'kindness'.
(Kate Dean)

. . . .

Recognising our woes and faults, let us sit quietly with those parts of ourselves which cause us discomfort, with a spirit of gentle understanding and forgiveness.
(Kate Dean)

. . . .

If you knew, as I do, the power of giving, you would not let a single meal pass without sharing some of it.
(The Buddha)[22]

. . . .

I believe that we should aim at leaving this life with the words 'I tried to contribute something and I hope that through my efforts the world is slightly better than when I found it'.
(Philip Buttinger)[23]

. . . .

An integral part of the spiritual quest and journey for me is how our essence – who we are – can avoid being metaphorically drowned by the adversity that life so frequently brings.
(Michael Allured)[24]

22   https://tricycle.org/article/family-dharma-the-joy-of-generosity
23   From *Reflections: An Anthology of Prayers, Meditations and Poems by Contemporary Unitarians* (Unitarian Worship Sub-committee, Essex Hall, 1979), p 35.
24   From a sermon.

… for the ultimate trick in life to get the hang of is the ability to smooth time's passage.
(Andrea Waddell)[25]

....

In reality, instant by instant each particle of the Universe lives and dies … to live again.
(Roohi Majid)[26]

....

I was silent; beauty is my need – a longing, a thirst, in a world of greed.
(Jean Wallis)[27]

Closing words: *Farewell Soul Deep* by Kate Dean

We have created a community, if only for a limited time, where we have found a circle of trust. May our *Soul Deep* connections continue and strengthen us for whatever we may encounter in the coming days, knowing that what we have shared and experienced has created a sacred bond.

A note for participants: what next?

You have completed eight weeks of *Soul Deep* – congratulations! We hope you have been nourished by the process. But your soulful experience doesn't have to end here. You and other members of your group may be asking 'What next?'

Through the engagement-group experience you will have got to know each other on a deep level, deeper than is possible in a brief conversation

---

25   Andrea Waddell, *Sounds of the Soul: Adventures in Time* (Scribbulations LLC, 2009).
26   *GGU Poets: An Anthology, Golders Green Unitarians,* 2015.
27   *GGU Poets: An Anthology,* Golders Green Unitarians, 2015.

over coffee. For sixteen hours you have probably shared aspects of your spirituality and soul journey that you have never shared with others, or perhaps never examined closely yourself.

Some or all members of your group may wish to continue meeting beyond the eight weeks of this course and yet feel challenged that there is no session plan for weeks 9, 10, 11 and beyond. With this in mind, we have thought about how we can help you take those first steps to continue spiritual explorations, as individuals and as members of a group.

Continuing the journey using the engagement-group approach

Soul Deep offers a ready-made structure and format that can be used for engagement groups to explore an aspect of spirituality in which they are interested. Now that you are familiar with the structure, you can continue by creating your own sessions. Here are some ways to discover new material and themes, and how to work with them:

1. **Harvest ideas for future sessions**. As a group, begin jotting down a list of topics and themes on aspects of spirituality that you would like to explore. You could see how they relate to the broad themes during the eight weeks and draw out some questions for discussion from there.

2. **Continuing the 'Common Bowl' approach.** Collect materials that you happen to come across that speak to you and may resonate with others in your group. Those materials might relate to one or more of the themes that you have already explored with your engagement group, or they might be aspects of spirituality not touched upon in the course. In this way, at the end of your eight weeks together you will already have a collection of resources to share and use if you wish to continue beyond an eighth *Soul Deep* gathering. The following Lindsey Press publications (all available via the website of the Unitarian General Assembly, https://www.unitarian.org.uk/) might be good sources of readings and discussion questions for future sessions:

- *Fragments of Holiness – for Daily Reflection* (edited by Catherine Robinson)

- *Carnival of Lamps: Words for Prayer and Reflection* (by Cliff Reed)

- *Cherishing the Earth – Nourishing the Spirit* (edited by Maria Curtis)

- *Living with Integrity: Unitarian Values and Beliefs in Practice* (edited by Kate Whyman)

- *Twelve Steps to Spiritual Health* (by David Usher)

- *Life Spirit: for Groups and Individuals Exploring Deep Questions* (by David Usher)

3. Work with themes that have emerged during the eight weeks. Your group may have found some themes particularly stimulating, or participants might have suggested other readings inspired by the material. These are natural topics and material to continue exploring. Completely new topics could also be added.

4. Return to work on the eight original themes. The weekly themes for *Soul Deep* are 'big' and can be worked on from a range of perspectives. So, having spent eight weeks together, there is no reason why your engagement group should not repeat the sessions. The readings and suggested activities are multifaceted, and we hope they lend themselves to different aspects of spiritual inquiry. You could either revisit the readings and activities already explored, but from a different angle, or use the extra readings and activities provided in the Appendices.

If you have found spiritual nourishment in being part of this *Soul Deep* course, we encourage you to use the materials in this book, the framework of the weekly themes, and the structure of each session as a way of going deeper, both alone and with those who share your spiritual journey.

If you have benefitted from the experience, please share it with others. You may decide that you would like to facilitate a *Soul Deep* course yourself. We encourage you to do so! The facilitators' guidelines in the next Part are there to help you.

Finally, thank you for engaging with the material found here. We hope it has challenged you, comforted you, helped you in your explorations, and inspired you by generating the potential healing power of the engagement-group experience that we have sought to model in this course.

Part 3: Facilitator's Guidelines

Introduction

Part 3 is intended to help facilitators of *Soul Deep* to get the most from the experience, both for themselves and for course participants. What you will find here:

1. Becoming a facilitator
2. Session structure and tips
3. Active (or 'deep') listening and loving speech
4. Dealing with group dynamics and challenges
5. Practical tips for running the course in person, and online considerations
6. Check-lists for each step of the way
7. Sample timetables with detailed timing

A sense of real connection during *Soul Deep* sessions is made possible by creating safe space, and this is what you will be doing as a facilitator. In this section we shall explore your role and consider the engagement-group approach more deeply. We will examine the structure of the sessions and focus on deep listening, and what to do when you encounter difficulties. We end with some useful check-lists to help you when preparing for each session, while conducting the session, and when reflecting on it afterwards.

The Unitarian way

As Unitarians, we draw wisdom from diverse sources, and as such we attract people with a wide range of views into our communities. This is why it is particularly important to encourage a respectful curiosity about all views. We do this by acknowledging them in a neutral way and by asking questions, if appropriate, to discover more about them.

---

1. Becoming a facilitator

Soul Deep works best with a clearly identified facilitator. A facilitator serves as a guide and host, helping participants to embark on a journey of self-awareness and spiritual growth. As the facilitator of a *Soul Deep* group, you also play an important leadership role in 'holding' the group, and upholding the engagement-group principles and covenant. A facilitator ensures that the session flows smoothly, while keeping track of time and ensuring that everyone's voice is heard. Pools of silence in the group will happen. It's not up to you to fill the airtime. To model the practice of deep listening, you should resist the temptation to fill silences with your own contributions and opinions. By adopting a 'less-is-more' approach to facilitation, you are making the space.

Using the resources in this book, you can create a safe and inspiring space for participants to share their thoughts and feelings and learn from each other.

When you create a new group, especially with unfamiliar faces, certain expectations may naturally arise. Even if you don't identify yourself as a leader elsewhere, within this context you are the leader and guide for this group. Your participants will look to you as the leader, regardless of your personal doubts or your perceptions of others' expertise. So try to relax and enjoy it!

The format of each session is designed to help you lead the group with confidence. It offers a simple framework which is flexible enough to be adapted according to the needs of the group, or in response to any last-minute issues.

As a *Soul Deep* facilitator, you are making a generous offer to serve the spiritual needs of your community. Remember that there is not one single way to fulfil this role. For instance, if you are a natural introvert, the qualities of listening and thoughtfulness can be especially useful in this setting.

If this is your first time in this role, it's natural to feel nervous, and it's easy to believe that everyone is scrutinising you. However, in reality, they are more likely to be focused on themselves and their own concerns. They look to you to perform this particular role, and we encourage you to believe in yourself!

TRY THIS: Buddy back-up (or co-facilitation)

You may find it less daunting to run a group if you have a buddy to help you. You can share the responsibilities of running the group between you. You can choose to take it in turns to run sessions, or divide the session tasks between you. It's a good idea to decide this beforehand while you are preparing each week's session, but allow some flexibility to swap roles as necessary during the session itself.

---

2. Session structure and tips

Each weekly session has roughly the same structure. This is outlined in Part I, in the section headed 'Using the "engagement group" approach'. (See pages 9–10.) Here is a more detailed description of each part of the structure, with extra tips for facilitators.

Opening rituals

We have found that people appreciate a familiar opening and closing practice for every session. The sessions usually begin with a chalice-candle lighting, followed by a reading. One practice that the group may wish to adopt after the first session is to take turns to read the opening/closing words, to help create a sense of group ownership of the space.

Tip

- You may find that the group naturally develops its own rituals, such as a favourite quotation or prayer to start each session. Prepare to be flexible if something more specific suits the group.

Check-in

The check-in is an opportunity for participants to say how they are feeling and tell the group about any practical or personal issues (such as a hearing or visual impairment). It's also a chance for people to lay down anything that is burdening their minds, before beginning their time together. The usual process is to go around the circle, taking turns to speak.

Check-in tips

- Remind participants of the 'pass' option, and encourage them to be comfortable with some silence, perhaps taking three deep breaths, between each check-in.

- You can pass round a special object so that people know when it is their turn to speak.

- A participant's check-in should not last more than a minute. The size of the group will determine how long each participant has to check in.

- If participants are speaking as they are ready, rather than going around the circle in turns, make a note (mentally or on paper) of who has spoken, so you can keep track and encourage those who have not yet spoken. This is especially important with online meetings.

Activity and response

The core of the session consists of one or two activities or readings which offer stimulus and inspiration for reflection, sharing, and group discussion. To hear a range of voices, we encourage you to invite different members of the group to read each week. Depending on the personalities of participants, you should decide with them whether to agree in advance who the readers will be for each session, or whether to be more spontaneous.

Tips

- Taking turns to speak. If your group prefers to be more spontaneous, you can encourage people to speak as they feel moved in response to a reading, or during an activity. They can do this while holding an object or not. Include some silence, perhaps asking them to take three deep breaths between each check-in.

- A longer reading can be divided between two or more readers. They should be invited in advance and should be given a chance to decline.

Break/music

Time for a pause from the words and an opportunity for a comfort break.

Tips

- This break is especially important for online groups that need a break away from their screens. It is also useful for any group meeting that lasts for more than an hour.

- Music can be played, using a portable music player or Bluetooth speaker. There are many useful playlists available through online streaming services such as Apple Music, Spotify, and YouTube.

Activity and deeper sharing

Each meeting includes an opportunity for the group to engage in a shared activity. The activity is placed after the second reading in each session (apart from Week 5, when it occurs after the first reading). The purpose of including an activity each week is to give participants a chance to share their thoughts, feelings, and/or experiences in smaller groups of three or four, and develop the practice of deep listening.

Tips

- There are a number of alternative readings and activities in Appendices (ii) and (iii) which you may choose to use instead of the ones suggested for the session. In choosing to do this, you should take account of the culture of the group. They may prefer longer readings, or a different balance of poetry and prose, or more interactive hands-on activities than are suggested in the outline for the session.

- As the facilitator you will need to keep time so that participants don't have to worry about timing themselves. Give an indication of how much time each participant in the small groups has for sharing, and how they will know to allow the next participant's sharing to begin.

- Remind participants that pauses and silence are a natural part of the process.

- Remind participants that in order to receive the full benefit of the 'deep listening' in this section, this is not a space for back-and-forth conversation and debate.

Check-out

This is a final opportunity for everyone to speak, to say something about their experience of the time spent together, or respond to another prompt in the session plan. There is a fine balance between the need to give every participant their voice and the need to keep the sharing reasonably brief. Participants may be tired at the end of the session, and you have made a commitment to end on time.

Tips

- Offer a pause and time to think before asking everyone to speak. You can count slowly to 30 in your mind, rather than using a timer.

- Remind people of the pass option; if they are feeling particularly emotional, they may welcome 'permission' not to say anything.

Closing

Closing rituals provide the balancing book-end to the opening, and then they end the session.

Tip

- You may choose to invite one of the group to read the closing words.

Optional homework

We have found that some groups relish 'homework', or preparation for the next session, while others are happy just to show up. If your group likes doing extra activities, you can ask them to read the text for the following week, or do one of the activities in Appendix (iii). If you do this, it is important to make sure you allow some time at the beginning of the next session to acknowledge and share a little of what they have done as homework.

Adapting sessions for your setting

You may already know the individuals in your group well; but if not, try to get a sense of what they would appreciate about a session. Are they more cerebral, keen to engage mentally with an interesting reading or poem? Or are they more experiential and would appreciate a more hands-on or heart-centred activity? More time for discussion – or fewer words? We have tried to include a range of stimuli in the main sessions, but we have also added alternative readings in Appendix (ii) and alternative activities in Appendix (iii).

Be aware that people process information differently. They are therefore likely to relate in different ways to the readings and activities offered. The level at which they engage will depend on the meanings and associations that they ascribe to them in the light of their life experiences, which, in other words, are the 'hooks' on which they hang the ideas that they encounter, including the insights that they hear by being a participant in the *Soul Deep* course.

As a facilitator it is important that you are aware of neurodiversity considerations: differences in brain function which affect the way that individuals function in everyday life. Some people have a neurotypical brain function, which means that they process information in a standard way. The brain functioning of neurodiverse people causes them to process information in ways that differ from what is considered typical. To make sure you cater for participants who are neurodiverse, here are some tips:

- Provide information ahead of time about what to expect – and then stick to it.

- Be explicit about the 'pass' option and make sure you mean it – no subtle pressure to contribute,

- If the course is being held online, allow 'camera-off' mode.

- Explicitly accept devices such as fidget toys which help some people to concentrate.

- Offer alternative ways to participate where appropriate: for example, some people might be strongly averse to activities that involve movement or artistic responses.

And remember that many things that are good for neurodiverse people are good for all people anyway!

Asking for feedback: likes and wishes

It's useful to ask for feedback, especially if you think that things might need to be changed. One way to do this is to ask during a 'check-out' about people's likes and wishes: something they liked about the session, and something they wish would be different.

Helping to continue connections beyond eight weeks

A well-bonded group may wish to continue meeting after the eight-week course. We have included extra suggestions for what is next on pages 81–84. A bonded group may well be able to meet without a facilitator – or one of the group may offer to take on the facilitator role.

3. Active (or 'deep') listening and loving speech

Practise deep listening: listen with both ears

We are fond of the saying 'You have two ears and one mouth for a reason!' We believe the world would be a better place if we all became better listeners. At a *Soul Deep* session we give each other the gift of our undivided attention. How many times have you been having a conversation with a friend and they don't seem to be quite paying attention? You suspect that at any moment they might reach for their mobile phone, or they suddenly say something which makes it apparent that they haven't been taking in what you have said. This is what we are trying to avoid when we come together in a *Soul Deep* group for mutual support in our quest for spiritual exploration and growth. We grow and develop as spiritual beings through our connection and relationship with each other.

Citing a Vietnamese saying, 'It costs nothing to have loving speech', the Buddhist teacher Thich Nhat Hanh translated the Fourth Precept of Buddhism like this: *'Aware of the suffering caused by unmindful speech and the inability to listen to others, I vow to cultivate loving speech and deep listening in order to bring joy and happiness to others and relieve others of their suffering.'*[28]

This is a good starting point for thinking about how we can gently facilitate the practice of deep listening in sessions. It may seem to be a high ideal to 'relieve others of their suffering', but we have to start somewhere! If one person's suffering is that they have been trying to work out how to have a difficult conversation with a family member,

---

28   THE-FOURTH-PRECEPT-by-Thich-Nhat-Hanh.pdf (stillnessspeaks.com)

the fact that you are giving them your time and your ears may well be what is needed to give them courage to continue on the right path.

During *Soul Deep* sessions there will be opportunities to share and reflect in small groups. The practice of deep listening is to give the other person our full attention, to put aside our own opinions on the subject, or our 'oh-I-had-the-same-problem' responses.

There is another technique which is very similar to deep listening, but more interactive. It works well in one-to-one situations or groups of three. By using an 'Active Listening' approach, you give the same mindful attention to what the other person is saying, but you may ask questions to draw out more information or enable the other person to think more deeply about what they are saying. The best are open questions that begin with 'what', 'which', 'why', 'when', 'where', or 'how'. This is because they require more than a yes/no answer. It's not necessarily about presenting 'helpful advice', although some gentle suggestions may be used – sparingly! Active listening is about recognising that the answers are within the person you are working with, yet they may not be immediately obvious, so your role is to help that person to uncover them.

Soul Deep sessions include some activities which require deep listening and active listening techniques. The session plans describe these activities in more detail.

4. Dealing with challenges and group dynamics

Start the first session by establishing a 'group culture', using a group agreement or covenant. This can help if problems arise later. See 'The importance of a group agreement or covenant' in Part I (pages 11–12). We welcome people from diverse backgrounds, so it's likely that each group will include different styles of behaviour. You may encounter someone who needs encouragement to speak up, and someone dominant who will need a gentle reminder that other people in the room also need time to speak. There could be a challenging member who finds it hard to follow instructions or to be asked to do something. All of these people should be treated with love and respect, although it is important not to allow challenging behaviour to damage the experience of other participants. You will need to judge the degree of firmness required to manage the behaviour. As the facilitator, you can model how members of the group should behave with each other.

The structure of the sessions will help you with this. By outlining at the start what will happen in the session, and reminding the group about the covenant that they have agreed on, you may be able to head off any possible difficulties or misunderstandings. If there is some difficult behaviour during the session, you can refer back to the covenant, to encourage an individual to alter their behaviour.

The *Soul Deep* course is designed to build over eight weeks. For participants to get the most out of it, we recommend that each course is run as a 'closed' group. In other words, once the course has begun, no new participants will join the course. Participants should make a commitment to attend every session unless there are good reasons for absence. The group dynamic that we are seeking to create – bonding, deep listening, feeling responsible to show up for each other – does not lend itself to a drop-in format.

One nuance to keep in mind is that it may be that someone signs up for the course and then for a good reason is not able to attend all the sessions. While you may wish to exercise some flexibility, especially if others on the course already know the new participants, you should be aware that once the group has bonded in the initial session, the addition of new participants may have a disruptive effect on the group.

As the course progresses, the general feeling in each session may vary. This could be due to a variety of factors, such as the particular subject matter under discussion, or tiredness, or a significant event that has occurred earlier in the day that has affected members of the group. As the facilitator it is important for you to be aware of any shifts and changes in the group dynamic and in individual participants' state of mind, and to continue being calm and friendly in order to smooth over any bumps.

Dealing with difficult behaviour

Although we hope that everyone's groups will run smoothly, it is useful to be prepared for challenges. When disruptive behaviour affects others, it's time to act. We have found that there are generally three types of people who can cause problems in group sessions.

1. **Disruptive/confrontational.** This person finds it hard to stick to the structure of the session. They want to send the conversation off in their own chosen direction, which might be off-topic. They may be critical of others, or have their own agenda, or generally dominate the conversation.

2. **Emotional/oversharing.** This person sees the group as an opportunity to share deeply personal information as a form of group therapy. They may cause an awkward atmosphere by the level of their sharing, becoming over-emotional or dominating the conversation.

3. *Non-stop talker.* This person treats the open-hearted nature of the group as an invitation to take centre stage and dominate the conversation.

You may see a pattern here. These people are not good listeners, and they tend to dominate the session with their behaviour. But please don't let this put you off! We need to talk about the very few disrupters whom you *may* encounter, while reminding yourself that the majority of your participants will be responsive to the needs of the group. There are a number of different approaches that you can use, based on the nature of the difficulty:

- **Ignore.** If the behaviour is only mildly annoying, you may be able to ignore it. Ensure that everyone is still able to be heard. If not, speak directly to the person who is being disruptive.

- **Bridge.** If someone is in full flow but you need to move the conversation on, try to find a point at which to jump in so that you can 'bridge' back to the topic. Interrupt if necessary – this is your prerogative as facilitator of the group! Take control of the session in a friendly, diplomatic way by saying, 'What you're saying reminds me of...', or 'Thanks for raising that point. I think we should return to...'. You can then shift the conversation back on course, according to the structure that you explained to everyone at the beginning of the session.

- **Challenge.** If someone is particularly disruptive, you may need to point out that the behaviour is not appropriate. If ignoring or bridging has not worked, and you are weary of speaking to the person in front of others, take them to one side to explain the situation. Tell them that you would like them to stay, if they are able to abide by the agreed covenant (of mutual respect); but if this is not possible, they will need to leave the session or the group entirely.

It is sad and upsetting if you have to reach the point of asking someone to leave. If possible, try to find a non-confrontational way to include the person who displays disruptive behaviour. This is because often the most resistant people are the ones who make the most progress, and perhaps that's because they have further to go. But it's important not to let them drain all your energy, or dominate the group to the extent that they silence and therefore potentially harm other members of the group. Small signs of progress need to be celebrated, as long as the behaviour is not causing other participants to suffer.

Sometimes, however, it's necessary to accept that some people just won't change, and actually it's not your job to make them change, anyway! If the behaviour is having a negative effect on the rest of the group, you have no choice but to deal with the situation and remove the person if necessary.

5. Practical tips for running the course in person – and online

Setting up the room for in-person sessions

You will need a circle of chairs and a table for your resources. If possible, allow extra space to spread out for smaller breakout-group discussions.

Preparing for the course

The Introduction to this book includes an outline of how the sessions are structured. We strongly encourage you to read each session and do any specified exercises beforehand, so you will feel comfortable explaining them to the group and are ready with answers to questions that participants might have. We have also made check-lists to help you to prepare for the course.

We recommend that you aim for a group of 8 – 12 people. The course will work with fewer people and is manageable with more, but we have found that this range provides enough diversity of voice to enrich discussions and still allows time for all voices to be heard. The group can then be divided into smaller groups of two or three for deeper, more intimate sharing and reflection.

Materials needed for each session: a chalice dish or candleholder, candle and matches (or a flame-free alternative), spare paper and pens (for in-person sessions), music player, a timer device, other materials as detailed in the session.

Online considerations

If you have decided to run the course using a video-conferencing platform such as Zoom or Teams, there are a number of extra issues to consider.

- **Video on or off?** It's useful to be able to note body language, but there may be a number of reasons why video is turned off: for example, a poor Internet connection. We recommend that video is turned on, to simulate an in-person gathering, unless there are valid reasons to keep cameras turned off.

- **Managing interactions and determining who speaks next.** With in-person groups, we are used to going around the circle taking turns to speak, but in an online meeting it's harder to work out who should speak next, so the process needs more intentional management. Interactions may be less spontaneous, and people may need to be invited to speak, or asked to raise their hand. Another method that we have used is to pass an imaginary 'ball' from one person to the next. After someone speaks, they choose the next speaker by saying 'I'll pass the ball to...'. However, some participants who experience anxiety are likely to feel uncomfortable by being 'put on the spot' in this way, and they will disengage emotionally, becoming increasingly anxious as they anticipate being passed the ball. We do not therefore recommend this method unless you know that all participants are genuinely comfortable with it (and not just going along with it). It helps if the facilitator keeps a note of who has spoken, to help the later participants to know who they can 'pass the ball' to.

- **Using the chat function.** An online meeting provides the added function of sending messages, but these can distract attention from the practice of deep listening. If you do decide to use it, we recommend that you do so to fulfil a particular purpose, and never for 'back and forth chat'. Agree at the beginning of the course how you would like to use the 'chat' function: for example, using the setting that means that messages are sent only to the facilitator.

- **Use of breakout rooms.** To make sessions run smoothly, ensure that you know how to set up and manage breakout rooms. Work out how to assign participants, and how long they will be in the breakout room.

- **Hybrid arrangements.** Hybrid sessions (simultaneously online and in-person) are not recommended for engagement groups. For facilitators to do the best job they can and to help everyone get the most out of the course sessions, we suggest that the meetings should be either in person or online. However, if a hybrid format is desired, we recommend having one online facilitator, with appropriate technical ability, and one in-person facilitator, so that the breakout sessions in smaller groups can be managed successfully. Allow extra preparation time, for example to set up a screen, and contingency time to manage technical difficulties, which can be frustrating for all concerned.

6. Check-lists for each step of the way

Here is a useful collection of check-lists. They will help you to ensure that everything is on track when you are preparing for the course, before each session, during each session, and afterwards. You might find it helpful to tick each box once you have completed that particular task.

Planning the course

☐ Know your purpose in offering the course. What do you want participants to gain from the experience?

☐ Is it intended for members of the existing congregation, or are you aiming it at newcomers or the wider community? Or a mixture of all three? What are you trying to create?

☐ Advertise in a range of places and talk about the course in a way that generates interest. Word of mouth is effective, so ask people to invite a friend.

☐ Have you decided to work with a co-facilitator?

☐ Will you offer the course online or in person? (See 'Online considerations' above.)

☐ Research the day/time that is likely to work best for potential participants.

☐ Encourage people to sign up/register, so you know who is coming, rather than allowing people just to turn up. Will it be a closed group where new people aren't admitted after the first session, or an open drop-in group? Open groups offer more flexibility, but we recommend closed groups, which promote deeper sharing.

☐ Be clear about expectations. Encourage people to sign up for the entire course and commit to attending every session.

☐ A week before the start of the course, send a welcome message to registered participants, with instructions for joining. Outline the course and its aims. State what materials they will need to bring, including a notebook and pen, and a copy of *Soul Deep*.

Before the session

☐ Send a reminder on the previous day.

☐ Consider assigning someone in advance to read aloud the key texts, to give them time to practise.

☐ Tell people what to expect, so that you manage expectations.

☐ Work out timings in relation to the number of people.

☐ Revisit the session and this chapter, even if it's just skimming particular sections yourself, so that you are prepared.

☐ If online, revisit the 'Online considerations' advice (above).

☐ Make sufficient copies of the Covenant template, with the rationale for each statement, for each member of the group (see Appendix (i)).

During the session

☐ Greet participants warmly, express gratitude for their presence, and maintain a welcoming atmosphere.

☐ Take the register so you know who attends.

☐ Don't assume that everyone knows each other's name. During the first session, attenders could say their name before speaking each time, and/or wear name labels.

☐ Manage expectations by reminding participants that the course is about deepening our spiritual exploration in community, but it is not a group therapy session, and that we get out of it what we put into it.

☐ Watch people's body language to gauge feelings/reactions.

☐ Ask whether participants want more time for sharing in the whole group.

After each session

☐ Follow up within 24 hours with a friendly message. We suggest an email thanking the participants for joining you, reminding them of anything they need to prepare for the next session, and encouraging them to continue reflecting on their spiritual journey in the coming days.

☐ Consider some self-reflection on how the session went. Debrief with your co-facilitator, if you have one.

☐ Begin to prepare for the next session!

7. Sample timetables with detailed timing

In Part 2 (Weekly Sessions), the content of each session is presented. It includes suggested timings for the main interactive elements, such as check-in, activities, breaks, and check-out. Below are more detailed timetables which facilitators may find useful. Week 1 and Week 8 use a slightly different format. The rest of the sessions have a similar structure to Week 2. These examples assume that the session runs from 6.30 pm to 8.30 pm.

Week 1

Time	Session component	Duration in minutes
6.30	Chalice lighting and silence	3
	Opening words	2
6.35	Check-in	15
6.50	Overview of course	10
7.00	Group agreement/covenant	10
7.10	Overview of session	2
	Reading 1	3
7.15	Group discussion	10
7.25	Break/music	10
7.35	Reading 2	5
7.40	Activity	10
7.50	Small-group sharing (groups of 3 or 4)	20
8.10	Announcements	2
	Check-out	10
8.22	Closing words	1
8.23	Contingency time in case of a late start	7

Week 2   (There will be similar timings for Weeks 3–7.)

Time	Session component	Duration in minutes
6.30	Chalice lighting and silence	3
	Opening words	2
6.35	Check-in	15
6.50	Overview of session	5
	Reading 1	5
7.00	Group discussion	10
7.10	Break/music	15
7.25	Reading 2	5
7.30	Activity	10
7.40	Small-group sharing (groups of 3 or 4)	25
8.05	Small-group responses shared with the larger group	5
8.07	Announcements	2
	Check-out	10
8.19	Closing words	1
8.20	Contingency time in case of a late start	10

Week 8

Time	Session component	Duration in minutes
6.30	Chalice lighting and silence	3
	Opening words	2
6.35	Check in	15
6.50	Overview of session	5
	Reading 1	5
7.00	Group discussion and check-out through closing reflections	20
7.20	Activity: farewell memory messages	20
7.40	Break/music	15
7.55	Closing ritual	25
8.20	Contingency time in case of a late start	10

Appendix (i): Group covenant

Group covenant with explanations

In early 2018, the organisers of the Unitarian Hucklow Summer School, a seven-day religious education retreat, held a 'Facilitation Summit' at which a group of experienced facilitators developed the following 'core covenants'. They are based on the ways of being together that over the years Summer School engagement groups had agreed at the start of their time together. A pattern of needs and wants appeared to emerge, and so, to make best use of time, the Summer School organising panel created a template. We offer these statements as a starting point for forming a covenant in your own engagement group.

The first column lists twelve suggested engagement-group commitments, and the second column explains the principles behind each of them. It is helpful to spend some time exploring and adapting these in your group, as this tends to create a greater sense of 'ownership': we find that group members are more likely to abide by covenants if they have fully understood and internalised the thinking behind them.

We will arrive on time and do our best to finish promptly too. We will come in quietly and take time to settle without chatting.	Our time together is precious, and the facilitators will have planned activities to fill the entire session, so we do not want to be waiting for latecomers, and we want to set the mood to go deep together.
We will take care to listen to others without interruption or cross-talk, without expressing judgement, or making personal comments (and we will not jump in with our own anecdotes or unsolicited advice when they've finished).	We want the group to be a space where people feel safe to share more deeply than they might in everyday conversation … and so we are trying to get out of everyday conversational habits.
We will allow people to talk about difficult situations/feelings without trying to 'fix them' (unless people have explicitly asked for help).	Parker J. Palmer says: 'When you speak to me about your deepest questions, you do not want to be fixed or saved: you want to be seen and heard, to have your truth acknowledged and honoured.'
We will use 'I-statements', speaking for ourselves, and not making generalisations / assumptions about others (i.e. avoid saying things like 'of course we all…' or 'you know when you…').	'I-statements' are a personal witness to your own life. Using them helps you to 'own' your own statements – with no implication that you are making assumptions or speaking for others in the group. Speak your truth: from your centre to the centre of the circle.

We will try to ensure that everybody gets a chance to be heard. Bear in mind that time is limited – we each need to monitor our contributions and take care that others have a chance to speak.	We value everybody's contribution, and it is important that more talkative members do not inadvertently dominate the group. Quieter members may need more space and time to contribute.
We will welcome moments of shared silence and will not rush to fill the silences with words (as we might do in everyday conversation).	Time to pause and reflect is precious. This is an opportunity to escape the pressure to 'keep up conversation' at all times.
We will take responsibility for how much we choose to share.	This is not a therapy group, and there is no pressure to reveal all!
We will not speak about other people's personal stories outside the group, or discuss things that people have said/done without their express permission, even if they seem innocuous. We can also refuse to reopen a conversation outside the session. It is fine to talk to others about the activities we have been doing in the group, or to speak about our own personal contributions – if this does not break any confidences of other group members.	Confidentiality matters in order for people to feel safe to open up and go deeper when sharing with others in the group. This is a delicate area and must be negotiated with care by all members. Consent is key. It is OK to ask for someone's permission to speak after the session about things they have said and done in the group, but it is also very much OK to refuse, and a 'no' should be respected. You may wish to explicitly state upfront, at the time of sharing, that you do not wish to discuss it at all after the session.

We respect one another's right to participate in ways that they feel are best for them, and at a depth which enables each one to get the most that they can out of the experience.	It may be that you are not in the right frame of mind for a particular activity – or that there are obstacles to your participation. If so, it may be possible to adapt the activity so that it works better for you.
We will take responsibility for self-care and remember to use the 'pass option' when we feel we need to (although you are encouraged to participate in the various activities, or at least 'give them a go' as much as you feel able to, to get the most out of the group).	We make the pass option explicit because sometimes knowing you don't 'have to' join in makes it more possible to 'give it a go'. Groups like this are a rare opportunity to go deeper, and we would like you to join in as much as you feel able to; but there is no obligation.
If at any point we find that we do not understand what is going on, or find the process unclear, we will ask for further clarification.	If one person finds something confusing, then it is likely that others do too, so this is potentially helpful for everybody!
If for some reason we cannot attend a session (e.g. we are unwell), we will send a message to the facilitators to let them know.	The group facilitators and participants will worry about you if you don't show up and they may be waiting for you before starting the session.

Group Covenant summary

- We will arrive on time and do our best to finish promptly too. We will come in quietly and take time to settle without chatting.

- We will take care to listen to others without interruption, cross-talk, expressing judgement, or making personal comments (and we will not jump in with our own anecdotes or unsolicited advice when they have finished).

- We will allow people to talk about difficult situations/feelings without trying to 'fix them' (unless they have explicitly asked for help).

- We will use 'I-statements', speaking for ourselves, and not making generalisations /assumptions about others (i.e. avoid saying things like 'of course we all ...' or 'you know when you ...').

- We will try to ensure that everybody gets a chance to be heard, bearing in mind that time is limited. We each need to monitor our contributions and take care to ensure that others have a chance to speak.

- We will welcome moments of shared silence and will not rush to fill the silences with words (as we might do in everyday conversation).

- We will each take responsibility for how much we choose to share.

- We will not speak about other people's personal stories outside the group, or discuss things that people have said/done without their express permission, even if they seem innocuous. We can also refuse to reopen a conversation outside the session. It is fine to talk to others about the activities that we have been doing in the group, or to speak about our own personal contributions – if this does not break any confidences entrusted to us by other group members.

- We respect one another's right to participate in ways that they feel are best for them, and at a depth which enables each one to get the most that they can out of the experience.

- We will take responsibility for self-care and remember to use the 'pass option' when we feel we need to (although everyone is encouraged to participate in the various activities, or at least 'give them a go', as much as they feel able to, to get the most out of the sessions).

- If at any point we find that we do not understand what is going on, or we find the process unclear, we will ask for further clarification.

- If for some reason we cannot attend a session (for example, if we are unwell), we will send a message to the facilitator(s) to let them know.

Appendix (ii): Extra readings

Using the extra readings

In the outline template for each of the eight sessions, we have offered two readings as inspiration for the shared and private reflection of participants, and as a focus for a shared activity. In addition we have been blessed with a wealth of enriching material in response to our call for contributions, so we have included this Appendix of extra resources, presented in accordance with the weekly themes.

We have sought to include a variety of poetry and prose contributions. We have also drawn inspiration from the contributions to design some extra activities in Appendix (iii). The additional readings included in this Appendix may be used in a variety of different ways:

- as alternatives to one or both of the suggested readings in one or more of the main outline templates;

- as resources for private reflection and appreciation.

When using the material for your own reflection, you may find value in reading a piece aloud. Or you may want to engage with the material as part of your regular or newly established spiritual practice. This could, for example, include journalling, meditating, drawing, or use of stream-of-conscious writing – a practice that allows you to respond instinctively to what you have read.

Another way of engaging with the material could be through the deliberate act of writing out a piece yourself, either on paper or electronically. See whether this practice deepens your understanding of the words.

You may of course be inspired to create other ways of using this additional material. If so, then we (the authors) will have fulfilled our purpose!

Week 1: Finding purpose, meaning, and identity

All That Is Our Life by Linda Hart

We come into the presence of all that is our lives,
here in these moments of calm and quiet
and mindful of the spirit of Love and Life
that inhabits every moment.

May we remember in these days
of the fullness of what we know
how joy becomes twined with sorrow,
how love brings tears to our eyes,
how sweetness can come in such strange guises.

The drift of our days
lulls us
allows us to forget
these things we know,
and sometimes we are startled by
the struggle of the ordinary,
the difficulty of what is simple,
sometimes we wish for what is easier,
what gives us less worry,
what offers calm and peace.

Help us, Spirit of Love,
to find the meanings that rest within it all:
that each of us brings our troubles and failings,
our frailties and sorrows,

and that love is everlasting,
never lost,
never gone,
always present.

Forgiveness is real,
Promise always beckons,
even in the presence of turmoil and loss.
May we remain in the presence of the love that abides,
and be awake to what is in our lives,
this day and every day.

Week 2: Our need for connection

'Forest' from Bold Antiphons *by Leonard Mason*

We pitched our tent beside a giant redwood. It was an open glade, but the eaves of the forest were near enough to be magnetic.

Great trees attract silence as a magnet iron filings. Our tent was in the field of their silence, so profound that I could not sleep for it. There were a faint moon and many stars. Often these have been companions of my vigil, but their influence was remote. It was the dark phalanx of the trees that gave the night its substance and brought two thousand years about my ears.

I heard the muted bourdon of the forest: some [people] come to be alone, some come to cut and haul away, some come to hide and some to hunt, some to carve a name and make furtive love, some to play Tarzan, some came tortured and hanged themselves, some were mercilessly strung from the hanging tree, some came to die with falling leaves for funeral.

Trees of the forest have welcomed all without blame, without judgement. They have seen everything before and are not buffeted.

When you come down aisles of soft tread and feel the Gothic architecture of the world, do not bow or genuflect. Stand and know yourself and a thousand other selves who have come and left their thoughts among the leaves.

Know the count of time, the bole-rings of the years. Know ages spanned by living arms that reach for light. Let [the] present pass while leaves sink silently. All your years are folding in your loam where other feet will softly tread.

Beyond the Green Doors by Aria Datta

From sizzling summer sun heat,
Through welcoming green doors,
A soothing waterfall of colour and light:
Dappled dream fawn-forest,
Green-gold grass, leaves;
Calm-blue water borders,
Dusky reddish-brown fruits, dotted white flowers.
Spirit of Wonder interlaced with Beauty.

Treading the footprints of questioning minds,
Birthing welcoming babies,
Blowing bubbles from the pulpit,
Hand linking hand, a family circle of support,
Exploring the unknown, changing perspective,
Celebrating our joy, embracing our pain,
Daring us to leave our imprint.

To see beauty in a vision as a reflection of the unseen,
To look upon a rose, absorb its deep aroma,
Petals, spiralling different colour shades:
Richness, creation, perfection
Converging to a single stem:
To see a rose as if for the first time.

Sitting on a garden seat,
Face out-turned towards the hills,
Summer evening rays warm wet lashes;
Suddenly that cutting edge of Beauty
Overwhelming my being: and I know that
'Apart' is 'part' if only the whole be defined.

To share in joyous comradeship,
To sing in spite of sailing off tune,
Secure with those who applaud the trying:
Sacred, seasonal circle dance,
Hands poised to give and receive,
Accepting that one cannot exist without the other,
Drawing awareness of the Dance interlacing our lives.

Earth, Energy, Santi.[29]

---

29 Santi means 'peace' in Bengali.

Week 3: The big questions

Part 1: Good, evil, suffering, faith, doubt, and the nature of God

The Power of Good by Michael Allured

What I believe about God is a work in progress. The biggest obstacle to believing in a benevolent God is the sheer amount of suffering in the world: human evil, like abuse or mass killing, and natural evil, like earthquakes.

I struggle because we know so little about this ineffable Being. Indeed, we don't know if God is a being or a process. The concept of God as a process feels nearer to my perception of reality. It may feel more nebulous than the greater certainty offered by organised and institutionalised religion. Yet, for me, it provides a foundation for exploring the possibilities of an Ultimate Universal Spirit.

And what of the 'Power of Good': the *yin* to the *yang*? It was a peace campaigner and humanist, Richenda Barbour, who helped me to gain perspective on the imponderable question of God's existence. 'I believe in a God with two Os', said this 'saintly' soul, who with her husband named their home in Golders Green 'World Government House'. It wasn't a grand gesture, just a longing for the peoples of the world to live in peace and global harmony. She and her husband Philip vowed to 'only have lodgers of colour' in times when racial discrimination was commonplace. Their Ghanaian lodgers and their children, one named Richenda after her, came to both their memorial services. They were there for that love nurtured by goodness.

One way of thinking about the Divine is perhaps to see God as the sum of all the good things in the world, and that we can affect the Spirit of God by nurturing and expanding our love and compassion. We cannot know a remote God in this life. But we can know and do tangible good. In this way we encourage 'the God within' to nurture the ways of empathy, compassion, and faith in the 'Power of Good'. We may be wrong, but it matters not. There is value in spelling God with two Os.

Kalighast[30] by Ayndrilla Singharay

The dirtiest place on earth
And I am in love with it.
What is this energy that flows through the mud-caked alleys?
I leave my *choti* with an old man and start walking barefoot through the slums.

It's hard to breathe sometimes,
The stench of life and death is too strong here.
At times the air is foul, at times its heady fragrance reawakens my spirit.
I clasp the most beautiful flowers in the centre of my left hand.

All categories of humanity are represented here,
In this heaving body of joy and suffering.
Faces I will never see again rush past me,
And silver coins are dropped into metal bowls held aloft by hardened hands.

---

30   Kalighast is an area of South Kolkata and is home to one of the most famous Kali temples in India.

Inside, my bare feet meet the cold floor.
Bells ring as a man I do not know recites prayers.
Words incomprehensible and yet more familiar than my own
name.
This man is not a priest and does not need to be.

A small donation to the men on the stage, and they perform a
miracle.
The dense mass of bodies is thrust aside and for the briefest of
moments.

The huge black-rimmed almond eyes of Kali stare into my soul.
For two rupees here you can see God.

A sliding thumbprint paints a third eye into my forehead,
An orange blessing, a tongue of fire,
Burning my body and my heart.
I step outside, where a small boy calls me 'Didi' and holds out his
tiny cupped hand.

Later, I notice my own flower-stained hands.
Those deep violet wounds of worship are still imprinted on my left
palm.

Week 4: The big questions

Part 2: The cycle/circle of life: birth, death, and everything in between

For Our Forever by Sally Somerville

We will treasure every pebble found on every walk
On every beach no matter where

And the mounting piles of greetings cards from countless years of
Valentines and birthdays
And tenderest goodbyes
From those who shared our griefs

For our forever
We'll be blest with memories of joys of sharing
Food and music, wine and laughter
Friends and films and walks
Hard work and holidays

And when we die
If one is left
to do it all alone
If our forever's yours
I will be there
In memory
Or you with me

Spring Comes to the City
by Du Fu (712 – 770 CE), a Chinese poet of the Tang Dynasty
Translated by Roger Mason

Our government has broken down,
Yet rivers flow and hills stand tall;
Deep grass and trees sprout in the town,
Spring flowers bloom, my sad tears fall,
And I startle at the cries of horrid crows.
Letters from home are like crocks of gold,
While for three months the warning beacon glows.
I scratch my scanty hair, and now I'm old,
On my white head it's got so thin
I've not enough to wrap around a pin.

Week 5: What gets in the way: spiritual baggage

Hold the Fire, Catch the Wind: Thoughts on Liberation – Learning to Let God be God by Judith Fantozzi

How shall I describe You, Spirit of our God?
    Hold the fire in a bottle
    Catch the wind in a cage
    The bottle breaks
    The wind blows free

Write Your Words upon a page
    The sages come
    The fools rush by
    And ever they will ask You why
    You hide Yourself intangible

Sign Your Name in flaming letters on the sky
The question marks
Of passers-by
Fill the air and queries flow
Of things that always have been so
And evermore shall be

I know more than I know I know
For your Spirit dwells in me
Knowing all things that were or are
And all that are to be
At any time to me to show
Anything I need to know

And so content in You I rest
The heart that loves You
Knows you best
And need not know Your form
More important far
To know that You know me.

Personally Transformative Prayer by Bert Clough

Prayer can be difficult for some Unitarians, particularly in the absence of a personal God – although I am sure some of us pray for a sermon to end. Do we Unitarians address our prayers to God, or to the Divine Spirit, or to the Nameless One? And if you post a letter addressed to 'whom it may concern' are you ever likely to get a reply?....

Maybe our most effective prayers are those that ask for nothing, but help us communicate with each other. They don't depend on supernatural intervention – a divine waving of a magic wand that will give us what we want, whether a toy for a child or the release of a loved one from terrible mental and physical suffering.

Perhaps God does not intervene tangibly in human affairs. Perhaps we ourselves are God's hands – not in his hands. ...

Maybe prayer can be personally transformative, rather than a petition to change external circumstances. Buddhists do not pray to an external God, but contemplate or meditate to awaken their own spiritual enlightenment, buried deep within them.

Week 6: What gets in the way: pressures of everyday life

On the Hook by Jane Blackall

Many of us are kept 'on the hook' by the economic necessities of our lives. For as long as we are embedded in a capitalist society – one which wants ever more of our time and energy – one which encourages the false belief that we should measure our worth by our productivity, and relies on an unhealthy culture, piggybacking on the vestiges of the protestant work ethic – while we're stuck in this culture, maybe our choices are somewhat limited. That's an unjust pressure coming from without, and one which we should collectively resist, but it's a reality we need to acknowledge. Having said that, we often have more choices than we think we do, and it's important to remember that as well. Letting ourselves 'off the hook' might be the hard choice rather than the easy one; there may be consequences, in this society that so often wants to use us up and burn us out for profit. But we don't have to accept and internalise those values. And for those of us who have more choices, those who have a bit of (relative) privilege, it's on us to keep our eyes and ears open to the pressures that keep others unjustly 'on the hook'. And do what we can to disrupt, overturn, or at least ameliorate them.

Leisure by W H Davies

What is this life if, full of care,
We have no time to stand and stare? —

No time to stand beneath the boughs,
And stare as long as sheep and cows:

No time to see, when woods we pass,
Where squirrels hide their nuts in grass:

No time to see, in broad daylight,
Streams full of stars, like skies at night:

No time to turn at Beauty's glance,
And watch her feet, how they can dance:

No time to wait till her mouth can
Enrich that smile her eyes began?

A poor life this if, full of care,
We have no time to stand and stare.

Week 7: Finding ways to deepen our soul connections

We Need a Church by Rory Castle Jones

Why are we here? Well, I think – at the risk of sounding a little dramatic – we are here to save the world ... We need a church where we can work in unison to prepare to help those hit hardest. We need a church to change the way our entire civilisation functions, as it destroys our world and itself in its relentless pursuit of profit. We need a church which is both sanctuary and prophetic, both a safe haven and a voice of protest. We need a church which can draw on several hundred years of loving community, and radical action – to hold aloft God's flame in the face of a world gone mad – and offer hope, offer love, and offer a vision of a world fundamentally and radically different from the one in which we live today.

Being the Answer to Big Questions by Michael Allured

What is life's purpose? Who am I, and where do I belong? Where am I going? What's my relationship to the Universe and the sentient beings in it? How are we as individuals – and as a circle of seekers – who embrace freedom, reason, tolerance, spirituality, and truth called to act in the world?

These are the big questions that can block or liberate our individual and collective spiritual journeys. These are questions of ultimate religious concern, which lead us to matters of discernment in how we judge what is true as we are overwhelmed with information and misinformation. For open minds, there is no single book containing all answers, no tablets of stone handed down to us. We have only our own hearts and minds and our communities shaped by the diversity of life experiences.

For me there's more: the possibility of the transcendent – that force, that mysterious mind behind the Universe. We seek and discover tentative answers through the insights, challenges, and wisdom revealed through being part of a liberal religious community, who love the questions and are learning to live with uncertainty. We encourage each other to use tender and generous hearts and reasoning minds to find and speak our truths in love. We live and love with our joys and sorrows, with our hopes and dreams, sometimes realised but often dashed. We are the bearers of each other's failings. This makes for an imperfect, bruised and aching world. Too many human eyes will not see, too many human ears refuse to hear. There are children on the world's streets now dying of starvation and other horrors. There are multi-billionaires who earn millions in 60 minutes, and people who live in destitution in refugee camps. How, as people of faith, recognising our interconnectedness in the web of life and believing in honouring the dignity of each person, should we respond to these injustices in the way we live our lives? For me, wrestling with all these questions and finding working answers is at the heart of what it means to live a religious life. We can be an answer to the big questions.

Note: There are no additional readings for the closing session, Week 8.

Appendix (iii): Extra activities

Week 1: Finding purpose, meaning, and identity

Additional information
Examples of a 'spiritual mission statement':

- 'I am the creative spirit that brings people together for mutual support.'

- 'I am the lively spirit that finds creative solutions to help others.'

- 'My place in the world is to use my helping hands to offer practical support to those in need.'

Activity: Tree of Life
Preparation for facilitators

You will need:

- An A4 or A3 sheet of paper for each participant

- Coloured pens or pencils, including plenty of greens and browns!

The narrative psychologist David Denborough illustrates the difference between focusing on the blessings in our lives and focusing on the blights in our lives:

> In all of our lives, there will be events that make us cringe, those that bring heartache, those that bring sorrow, those that bring shame. If those moments are all linked together into a storyline, we can feel truly hopeless about life. But in all of our lives, there

will also be events or small moments of beauty, or kindness, or respite, or escape, or defiance. When these events are linked together to tell a story about us, then life becomes easier to live.

Ncazelo Ncube-Mlilo used a 'tree of life' exercise, created by Denborough, when working with vulnerable children in South Africa. This approach is intended to emphasise positive strengths and inner resources.

☐ Invite everyone to try drawing a 'Tree of Life' with roots, a solid trunk, branches, leaves, and fruits.

☐ And then to label each part with examples from their lives:

- The roots: parents/grandparents/ancestors, family origins, community or area

- The ground: typical daily activities, occupation, chores

- The trunk: skills

- The branches: hopes, dreams

- The leaves: important people

- The fruits: gifts received from others[31]

☐ Finally, invite each of them, in discussion with other members of the group, to use their drawing to help them consider their own life; and help each other to do the same, by asking 'thickening questions': for example, 'Can you tell me more about ...'; or 'I noticed that ...'; or 'What made you include...?'.

---

31 https://www.crs.org/sites/default/files/tools-research/tree-of-life.pdf

Week 2: Our need for connection

Activity: Inspired by Wang Wei
Preparation for facilitators

You will need:

• A notebook or paper and a pen for each participant

This is a translation by Roger Mason of a poem by the 8th-century Chinese poet, Wang Wei. Wang places himself in the world by identifying his absence from the lives of his brothers.

Thinking of my brothers on the Double Ninth

A lonely stranger in a distant land

On each feast day my kindred fill my thought,

Atop a distant peak my brothers stand

With fragrant willow twigs, but one man short.

☐ Invite participants to write about how their sense of connection (or lack of it) with members of their family contributes to their sense of identity, and perhaps to their spiritual life.

Week 3: The big questions

Part 1: Good, evil, suffering, and the nature of God

Preparation for facilitators

You will need:

- A notebook or paper and a pen for each participant

Terry Waite is a humanitarian and writer. As an assistant to the Archbishop of Canterbury in the 1980s, he travelled to Lebanon on a mission to secure the release of four hostages and was himself kidnapped and held hostage in solitary confinement for five years. In an interview later he talked about how in survival mode he would tell himself Biblical stories that he knew by heart, and how they – and his faith – were part of his toolkit for his mental survival.

☐ Invite participants to write a reflection on what has helped them and continues to sustain them in times of adversity. If they wish to express their reflections through another medium that works for them (for example, drawing, meditation, looking at the natural world), that's all right too.

Week 4: The big questions

Part 2: The cycle/circle of life: birth, death, and everything in between

Activity: Starry Sky memories
Preparation for facilitators

You will need:

- A notebook or sheet of paper and a pen for each participant

Here is a stanza taken from 'Starry Sky', a longer poem by the 20th-century Chinese novelist, poet, and woman of letters, Bing Xin, and translated by Roger Mason.

> O childhood!
> Reality amidst a dream,
> and a dream amidst reality
> that leaves tearful smiles in memory.

☐ Ask participants if they have dreamy memories of childhood. What aspects of their younger selves do they find themselves returning to as they grow older? Invite them to address these questions by writing, drawing, or contemplating their own responses, before sharing in small groups.

Week 5: What gets in the way: spiritual baggage

Activity: What does God look like?
Preparation for facilitators

You will need:

- A sheet of A4 paper for each participant, and pens.

- A range of colourful pens is ideal, but one pen or pencil for each person is enough.

Unitarians have many different concepts of God. Most are indescribable or invisible. Yet we may still retain images of the divine from our previous religious tradition or upbringing which are worth exploring. In this light-hearted activity, each member of the group will create a combined image of the God of their childhood. It's fun and suitable for those with even the most basic of drawing skills. If the idea of drawing an image of God does not appeal, the group could decide to adapt the activity to create an image of a 'benevolent creature' or an angel.

☐ If they are happy with the proposal, take them through the following sequence of instructions.

- Take a sheet of paper and imagine that it is divided into four sections (see Diagram 1). Then draw a head with a neck.

- Fold down the top of the paper so that it covers the head, but leave the two lines of the neck showing (see Diagram 2).

- Pass the paper to the person on your left.

- Next, draw the torso and arms, and fold over the paper, leaving two lines at the waist point.

- Pass the paper to the person on your left.

- Now, draw the lower part of the body, including stomach,

pelvis, and hips, and then fold the paper down, leaving four lines for the tops of the thighs.

- Finally, draw the legs and feet and fold the paper up completely.

- When you receive the finished picture, unfold the paper and take a few moments to look at the image. (See Diagram 3 – for illustrative purposes only!)

- Write some words on the page. This could be a title, a phrase of response, or even a speech bubble.

- **Small-group sharing:** in small groups, share the image and your response to it.

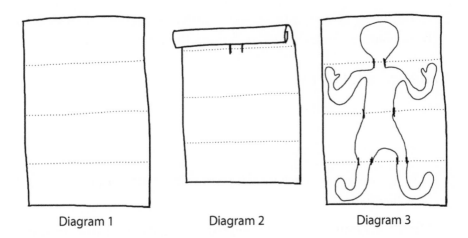

Diagram 1   Diagram 2   Diagram 3

Online adaptation (1)

This adaptation does not require any materials or drawing.

☐ Invite participants to take turns to describe the image as follows:

- Person 1: The head of God is ....

- Person 2: The torso and arms of God are ....

- Person 3: The stomach and pelvis of God are ...

- Person 4: The legs of God are ...

- Person 5: This image of God prompts me to say ...

☐ Repeat the process until everyone has spoken.

☐ Continue to 'go around the circle' until the final image of God has been completely described, including the final 'speech bubble'.

Online adaptation (2)

☐ Invite group members, using a thick pen, to draw an image of God from their childhood and an image of the divine from their current spiritual thinking.

☐ If images don't arise easily, they can write words or phrases to describe their concept.

☐ Show the group your own image and describe it for further clarity.

Week 6: What gets in the way: pressures of everyday life

Activity: Tea-break for the mind
Preparation for facilitators

You will need:

- a bell or singing-bowl

We are often constantly busy. We are buffeted from one task to another, sometimes to the extent that we are so caught up in the doing that we neglect to slow our whole selves down to simply be. During the Covid pandemic Michael Allured began offering to his Civil Service colleagues a daily online meditation / mindfulness session. He called these sessions, which were intended to help his colleagues pause and enjoy being still for 30 minutes, 'a tea-break for the mind'.

You might like to try this approach as a way of helping participants to calm their minds and allow themselves to simply be with the stillness.

☐ Gently chime a bell, and then use the following words:

- Take a few moments to find a comfortable position in any way that suits you.

- Bring your attention gently to your feet, and take some time to notice the points of connection between your feet and the ground.

- Gradually begin to notice the point of connection between your sitting-bones and the chair or ground.

- Now notice the connection of your upper body to the chair or the ground, and gently and gradually extend your attention to your neck and head.

- Notice the way in which the chair or the ground is supporting the weight of your body.

- When you are ready, bring your attention to the rhythm of your breath and take a few moments to notice how your breath feels.

- Gradually begin to notice the sensation of your breath within your body, paying attention to the sensation that it creates on the inner and outer breath.

- You are encouraged to take your time with this stage and to allow yourself to be with your breath, making it the centre of your world.

- Gradually you may extend your awareness to any sense of stillness in your immediate space. Perhaps you will notice sounds, while all the time staying with the rhythm of your breath.

- Continue with this practice for as long as it feels comfortable. Acknowledge any intrusive thoughts that come, and bring your attention gently back to your breath.

- This is your time. You do not need to do anything or be anywhere for the time that you have deliberately gifted to yourself for slowing down body and brain through simply noticing the breath. This is your tea-break for the mind.

Week 7: Finding ways to deepen our soul connections

Activity: Reflecting on Kindness by Kate Dean
Preparation for facilitators

You will need:

- Spare paper and pens for any participants who haven't brought a notebook.

A Jewish friend once asked me, 'At the end of your life, how are you going to know if you've been a good Unitarian?' From his point of view, being a good Jew required adherence to certain practices and abstaining from others. It is a sort of religious obligation that might not appeal to some liberal spiritual people. However, there is also something to be said for self-discipline that is chosen and enhances your spiritual life. When I was thinking of being a good Unitarian, the one word that came to mind was 'kindness'. I agree with Wordsworth, who honoured 'that best portion of a good man's life: his little, nameless, unremembered acts of kindness and of love'.[32]

The Prophet Mohammed said: 'You must be gentle. Whenever there is gentleness in some matter, it adorns it; and whenever it is taken away, it disfigures it.' In our rush to do everything at once, or even just to get to work on time, we may forget this universal truth: whenever there is gentleness in some matter, it adorns it, and whenever it is taken away, it disfigures it.

---

32   From *Lines Composed A Few Miles Above Tintern Abbey* (1798).

☐ Invite members of the group to reflect on a time recently when they have practised kindness or gentleness towards themselves or another person.

☐ Invite everyone to consider a time when this gentleness has been taken away. What lessons can be drawn from that experience?

Additional activity

Following the reading on Humility by Celia Cartwright, invite participants to consider these questions:

☐ Have you ever had a 'humbling experience'? Reflect on a time when you practised humility or witnessed it in others. Free-write, draw, or meditate on this aspect of the human experience and how it relates to your spiritual approach.

Week 8: Wrap-up: gathering, and bringing in the harvest

Activity: Closing Ritual

This is a group activity to co-create a closing ritual. If the group has bonded particularly well and has developed the practices of suggesting and sharing resources, this closing ritual can enrich their experience and offer them an opportunity to contribute creatively. Each participant offers words or music and helps to create a central 'altar' on which to place special objects, decorations, and candles.

Preparation for facilitators

At the end of the Week 7 session, ask everyone to bring materials in order to prepare for the Week 8 Closing Ritual. These should include the following:

- Their special object from Week 1, or another significant object.

- A meaningful piece of writing or music. The text should be a short paragraph and can be from this book or from another source. The piece of music should be no longer than four minutes.

- Other decorations for the 'altar' such as a scarf/table cloth, flowers or leaves, stones, bark, other natural materials.

- One tealight or small candle per person.

At the start of the session, cover a table to make an altar or focal point.

Closing ritual

☐ Begin with music.

☐ You may choose to use *When we are together in a circle of trust* by

Michael Allured from the Week 8 session (pages 74–75) as your opening reading, and the Closing Words by Kate Dean (page 81) at the end of the ritual.

☐ Invite everyone to place their objects and other decorations on the altar.

☐ Allow participants to make their contributions of words and music, leaving pauses between each sharing.

☐ Once everyone has shared, invite them to light a candle in turn and say a word or phrase to express their gratitude to the group.

☐ End with music.

Additional activity: A postcard to your future self
Preparation for facilitators

You will need:

• Blank postcards or envelopes; pens; stamps

☐ Explain that everyone is going to receive a postcard from themselves in two months' time.

☐ Give each person a postcard or sealed envelope, pen, and stamp.

☐ Ask them to imagine receiving the postcard and write an encouraging message to their future selves.

☐ Each person writes their address on the postcard (or sealed envelope) and affixes a stamp.

☐ The facilitator collects the postcards and makes a commitment to send them in two months.

☐ Alternatively, each person can take someone else's postcard, making a commitment to remember to send it in two months' time.

Appendix (iv): Sample promotion text

You could use the following text as a template to make a poster or social-media post to promote the course.

Soul Deep: Exploring Spirituality Together

An 8-Week Spiritual Development Course

Dates:

Location:

Join us for a weekly spirituality course, online/in person, led by [name] to deepen your spiritual awareness and connect with like-minded spiritual seekers. Each week we will explore a different theme through poetry, stories, and questions to reflect on in small groups.

Contact [name] for more details: [contact details]

Appendix (v): Sample follow-up invitation

Dear ....

Thank you for expressing interest in joining our new *Soul Deep* engagement-group course, consisting of eight two-hour weekly gatherings.

You will be part of a small group exploring your own and each other's experiences, beliefs, and questions of faith and doubt.

Here is the course plan:

[list dates and times]

- Week 1: Finding purpose, meaning, and identity

- Week 2: Our need for connection

- Week 3: The big questions, part 1: good, evil, suffering, and the nature of God

- Week 4: The big questions, part 2: the cycle/circle of life: birth, death, and everything in between

- Week 5: What gets in the way: spiritual baggage (how perceptions of God can be barriers on our spiritual journey)

- Week 6: What gets in the way: pressures of everyday life (time, finance, health, work–life balance)

- Week 7: Finding ways to deepen our soul connections: what we need to commit to do with others, as individuals and in a community

- Week 8: Wrap-up: gathering and bringing in the harvest.

To register for the *Soul Deep* engagement group, please contact:

....

Please note that you will need to invest in a personal copy of the book *Soul Deep* (available from the General Assembly website (www.unitarian.org.uk); or direct from Unitarian headquarters at Essex Hall: tel. 0207 240 2384).

At our first gathering please also bring ... *[this depends on the setting, for example, a snack, an extra cushion, etc.].* You will also find it helpful to bring a notebook and a pen.

I/we look forward to our time together. Please get in touch if you have any questions.

Signed: ....

Name: ....

Email: ....

Phone number: ....

Appendix (vi): Contributors

Yvonne Aburrow has an MA in Contemporary Religions and Spiritualities from Bath Spa University and has written four books on mythology and folklore, the latest of which is *Changing Paths*.

Jane Blackall, minister with Kensington Unitarians, is positively evangelical about the transformative power of engagement groups and created 'Heart and Soul' circles as a contemplative spiritual gathering where people can share deeply about their lives.

Jeffrey Bowes has served as the minister with Coventry Unitarians since 2009. He currently serves as the chair of trustees on the boards of the Retired Ministers and Widows Fund and the Ministers' Pension Fund.

Celia Cartwright retired from active ministry in 2016 and served as President of the General Assembly of Unitarian and Free Christian Churches from 2019 to 2021.

Rory Castle Jones, the minister of Gellionnen Chapel, is also the communications officer for the General Assembly of Unitarian and Free Christian Churches. He holds a doctorate in history and before entering the ministry he worked in higher education.

Bert Clough, a self-confessed 'lapsed atheist', published a collection of his sermons, *Dancing with Mortality: Reflections of a Lapsed Atheist* in 2020.

Aria Datta, a member of Golders Green Unitarians since the 1970s, still expresses wonder at finding Nature's phenomena in an equation or a poem.

Judith Fantozzi, a member of Golders Green Unitarians and keen actor, has written poetry for over 30 years.

Winnie Gordon, minister with Birmingham and Kidderminster Unitarians, first walked into a Unitarian church in 2006.

Linda Hart, a Unitarian Universalist minister who once served as minister of Richmond Unitarians, holds a doctorate in ministry.

Jo James, the Unitarian minister of Mill Hill Chapel, Leeds, serves on the Executive Committee of the General Assembly of Unitarian and Free Christian Churches and before ministry worked for more than twenty years in theatre.

Roohi Majid, a Muslim friend of Golders Green Unitarians, is a published poet, teacher, and translator and holds a doctorate in education.

Roger Mason is a retired geologist and member of Rosslyn Hill Chapel.

Ayndrilla Singharay is a playwright, screenwriter, and poet. Her play *Unsung* was performed to critical acclaim at the Edinburgh Fringe Festival 2014.

Adam Slate holds spiritual dual citizenship in the Unitarian and Unitarian Universalist traditions and is committed to building connections within and between congregations, social equity and justice work, and sharing Unitarian values with the wider world.

Jean Wallis, until her death, was a Friend of Golders Green Unitarians.

Milton Keynes UK
Ingram Content Group UK Ltd.
UKHW020107230224
438319UK00002B/183